APR 0 3 2001

CliffsNotes™

Shaara's
The Killer Angels

By Debra A. Bailey

IN THIS BOOK

- Learn about the Life and Background of the Author

- Preview an Introduction to the Novel

- Explore themes, character development, and recurring images in the Critical Commentaries

- Examine in-depth Character Analyses

- Acquire an understanding of the novel with Critical Essays

- Reinforce what you learn with CliffsNotes Review

- Find additional information to further your study in the CliffsNotes Resource Center and online at www.cliffsnotes.com

IDG
BOOKS
WORLDWIDE

IDG Books Worldwide, Inc.
An International Data Group Company
Foster City, CA • Chicago, IL • Indianapolis, IN • New York, NY

About the Author

Debra Bailey is a freelance author and editor in Cary, N.C.

Publisher's Acknowledgments

Editorial

Project Editor: Kelly Ewing
Acquisitions Editor: Greg Tubach
Editorial Administrator: Michelle Hacker
Glossary Editors: The editors and staff of Webster's New World Dictionaries

Production

Indexer: York Production Services, Inc.
Proofreader: York Production Services, Inc.
IDG Books Indianapolis Production Department

CliffsNotes™ Shaara's *The Killer Angels*
Published by
IDG Books Worldwide, Inc.
An International Data Group Company
919 E. Hillsdale Blvd.
Suite 400
Foster City, CA 94404

www.idgbooks.com (IDG Books Worldwide Web site)

www.cliffsnotes.com (CliffsNotes Web site)

ISBN: 0-7645-8549-5

Printed in the United States of America

10 9 8 7 6 5 4 3 2 1

1O/TQ/QV/QQ/IN

Distributed in the United States by IDG Books Worldwide, Inc.

Library of Congress Cataloging-in-Publication Data
Bailey, Debra A.
CliffsNotes The Killer Angels / by Debra A. Bailey.
p. cm.
Includes index.
ISBN 0-7645-8549-5 (alk. paper)
1. Shaara, Michael. Killer Angels--Examinations--Study guides. 2. United States--History--Civil War,1861-1865--Literature and the war. I. Title: The Killer Angels. II. Title
PS3569.H2 K553 2000
813'.54--dc21   00--038865
                                        CIP

Distributed by CDG Books Canada Inc. for Canada; by Transworld Publishers Limited in the United Kingdom; by IDG Norge Books for Norway; by IDG Sweden Books for Sweden; by IDG Books Australia Publishing Corporation Pty. Ltd. for Australia and New Zealand; by TransQuest Publishers Pte Ltd. for Singapore, Malaysia, Thailand, Indonesia, and Hong Kong; by Gotop Information Inc. for Taiwan; by ICG Muse, Inc. for Japan; by Intersoft for South Africa; by Eyrolles for France; by International Thomson Publishing for Germany, Austria and Switzerland; by Distribuidora Cuspide for Argentina; by LR International for Brazil; by Galileo Libros for Chile; by Ediciones ZETA S.C.R. Ltda. for Peru; by WS Computer Publishing Corporation, Inc., for the Philippines; by Contemporanea de Ediciones for Venezuela; by Express Computer Distributors for the Caribbean and West Indies; by Micronesia Media Distributor, Inc. for Micronesia; by Chips Computadoras S.A. de C.V. for Mexico; by Editorial Norma de Panama S.A. for Panama; by American Bookshops for Finland.

For general information on IDG Books Worldwide's books in the U.S., please call our Consumer Customer Service department at **800-762-2974.** For reseller information, including discounts and premium sales, please call our Reseller Customer Service department at **800-434-3422.**

For information on where to purchase IDG Books Worldwide's books outside the U.S., please contact our International Sales department at **317-596-5530** or fax **317-572-4002.**

For consumer information on foreign language translations, please contact our Customer Service department at **1-800-434-3422,** fax 317-572-4002, or e-mail rights@idgbooks.com.

For information on licensing foreign or domestic rights, please phone **+1-650-653-7098.**

For sales inquiries and special prices for bulk quantities, please contact our Order Services department at **800-434-3422** or write to the address above.

For information on using IDG Books Worldwide's books in the classroom or for ordering examination copies, please contact our Educational Sales department at **800-434-2086** or fax **317-572-4005.**

For press review copies, author interviews, or other publicity information, please contact our Public Relations department at **650-653-7000** or fax **650-653-7500.**

For authorization to photocopy items for corporate, personal, or educational use, please contact Copyright Clearance Center, 222 Rosewood Drive, Danvers, MA 01923, or fax **978-750-4470.**

Table of Contents

How to Use This Book

CliffsNotes Shaara's The Killer Angels supplements the original work, giving you background information about the author, an introduction to the novel, a graphical character map, critical commentaries, expanded glossaries, and a comprehensive index. CliffsNotes Review tests your comprehension of the original text and reinforces learning with questions and answers, practice projects, and more. For further information on Debra Bailey and *The Killer Angels,* check out the CliffsNotes Resource Center.

CliffsNotes provides the following icons to highlight essential elements of particular interest:

Reveals the underlying themes in the work.

Helps you to more easily relate to or discover the depth of a character.

Uncovers elements such as setting, atmosphere, mystery, passion, violence, irony, symbolism, tragedy, foreshadowing, and satire.

Enables you to appreciate the nuances of words and phrases.

Don't Miss Our Web Site

Discover classic literature as well as modern-day treasures by visiting the Cliffs-Notes Web site at www.cliffsnotes.com. You'll find interactive tools that are fun and informative, links to interesting Web sites, and additional resources to help you continue your learning.

You'll also find interactive tools that are fun and informative, links to interesting Web sites, tips, articles, and additional resources to help you, not only for literature, but for test prep, finance, careers, computers, and Internet too. See you at www.cliffsnotes.com!

LIFE AND BACKGROUND OF THE AUTHOR

Personal Background

"I wrote only what came to mind, with no goal and little income, always for the joy of it, and it has been a great joy." To Michael Shaara, the joy of carefully crafting a great story meant more than a mass-market audience or a lot of money. What hooked him was the fun of the story "waiting to be told."

Michael Shaara was born in Jersey City, New Jersey, on June 23, 1929. His father, Michael Joseph Sr., was an Italian immigrant active in local unions and politics. Shaara described his father as being similar to Shakespeare: "political, but no good with money." His mother, Alleene Maxwell Shaara, provided the opposite perspective in life. She was from the South, with family roots going back to Thomas Jefferson and "Light-Horse Harry" Lee. The diversity in his parents brought him in touch with both worlds, North and South, a factor that probably allowed him to understand both sides in the Civil War.

Education

Shaara did extremely well in school, winning more awards in high school than any other student in the history of the school. He received letters for basketball and track and excelled as a baseball pitcher. His father also taught him to box, something that remained a passion in his life and figured in his writing. Of the 18 matches Shaara fought as a young man, he won 17. The one loss would serve as the basis for a later short story, "Come To My Party."

Early Work

After high school, Shaara's work experiences resembled those of one of his favorite authors, Ernest Hemingway. Shaara served as a paratrooper for the 82nd Airborne Division, a merchant seaman, and police officer walking a beat. He married in 1950, graduated in 1951 from Rutgers University with a bachelor's degree and then did some graduate work at Columbia University and the University of Vermont. He spent the remainder of the 1950s working as a short story writer, predominantly in the science-fiction genre.

In 1961, Shaara accepted a position at Florida State University in Tallahassee, teaching creative writing and literature. It was probably a natural choice given his writing career, and he observed that he enjoyed teaching because "it taught him a lot." He worked hard at the challenge of reaching all of his students, describing the mix as "students with talent and no desire; desire and no talent; and a little of each." They responded by voting him Outstanding Teacher of the Year in 1967, earning him the Coyle Moore Award. He served there until 1973.

Michael Shaara wrote more than 75 short stories in his life. They were published in a variety of magazines, including *Astounding Science Fiction, Galaxy, Playboy, Cosmopolitan, Redbook,* and others. They covered a wide range of subjects, though the predominant one was science fiction.

Another popular theme with Shaara was boxing. "Come To My Party" is one of his better known stories in this vein. It is about a boxer who loses a prizefight because the opponent manages to avoid him in the ring, yet wins by the rules. It is based on Shaara's one loss to a fighter who "boxed, but couldn't hit." The boxer spent most of the fight avoiding Shaara and winning the match "on the rules." Shaara later observed that the man "would never have won in natural life, in a fight in a bar."

While teaching in Florida, Shaara used the boxing theme again in his first novel, *The Broken Place.* Published by New American Library in 1968, it is the story of a Korean War veteran, Tom McClain, seeking to be free of his demons and finding that freedom through his boxing. Shaara came back to his science-fiction roots in his third novel, *The Herald,* published by McGraw-Hill in 1981. The story has been described as more of a long short story than a novel. In 1982, Pocket Books published *Soldier Boy,* a collection of Shaara's short stories from the 1950s.

It was Michael Shaara's second novel, though, that brought him critical recognition, and its subject was a departure from both science fiction and boxing. *The Killer Angels* was a historical fiction about Gettysburg. Shaara's change in genre had a double catalyst: old letters and a vacation trip. The letters were from Shaara's great-grandfather, a member of the 4th Georgia Infantry, who had been injured at Gettysburg.

Seeking to learn more about his great-grandfather's experiences there, Shaara took a family trip to Gettysburg in 1966. His son, Jeff, who was 14 at the time, explained that his father "had a bad heart and could not climb the hills, so he would send me up there to describe them to him. . .It was probably the best time in my life with my father." The two returned in 1970 to finish the research, and it was published in 1974 by David McKay, after 15 rejections by other publishers.

The book's genius is in Shaara's ability to narrow down a huge subject to a few people and events that could make it personal for the reader. Shaara's background provided the insight to see both sides of the conflict. The results are crisp characters, vivid images, and an objectivity that avoided making heroes out of one side or the other.

It won the Pulitzer Prize in 1975, but there was not much public acclaim because it came out during the Vietnam War, a bad time for a war novel. Fame would not come until much later, five years after Shaara's death, when the film based on his book was released.

Final Years

A quote in Hemingway's book *A Farewell To Arms* inspired the title for Shaara's first book, *The Broken Place*. "The world breaks everyone and afterward many are strong at the broken places. But those that will not break it kills." Perhaps that quote best sums up the last years of Shaara's life.

Shaara was in a motorcycle accident in Italy in 1972, remaining in a coma for several weeks. The pain and stroke-like symptoms that resulted left him unable to concentrate and impaired his ability to write. Things seemed to go poorly after that.

In a 1982 interview he spoke of being similar to Shakespeare in that each had been married to the same woman for 30 years but became involved with a "Dark Lady," and each had lost a son. It was an odd comment, especially the last part, because his son Jeff, born in 1952, was still alive. However, it reflected reality. Shaara had divorced his wife in 1980 and had also severed all connections with his son.

For the remaining years of his life, the active and talented man who had done so much and written so well, was restricted by health problems. He was able to write his third novel, *The Herald*, as well as a screenplay for *The Killer Angels*. He also traveled to Ireland to do some site research for the filming of that screenplay, but his health continued to hamper his activities. Unable to enjoy so many things that had given him joy — including his writing — he was bitter and withdrawn. Michael Shaara died on May 5, 1988, at the age of 59.

At the time of his death Shaara left behind a number of projects. These included an autobiography, the screenplay for *The Killer Angels*, a book on Shakespeare, and an unpublished novel about baseball, written several years earlier. His son, Jeff, took over his literary estate and brought about the posthumous publication of the baseball novel, *For Love of the Game*, which was later made into a movie starring Kevin Costner. Even more importantly, working with an old friend of his father's, Ronald F. Maxwell, Jeff Shaara saw to it that the screenplay for *The Killer Angels* made it to film. In 1993, with Maxwell as director, the film, *Gettysburg*, was completed. Following a suggestion from Maxwell, the younger Shaara, took on the challenge of completing a trilogy that had his father's book, *The Killer Angels*, as the centerpiece. Jeff Shaara wrote *Gods and Generals*, set before *The Killer Angels*, and *The Last Full Measure*, set right after it.

INTRODUCTION TO THE NOVEL

Introduction

The book tells the story of the Battle of Gettysburg, attempting to present both a factual retelling of events as well as the emotional experience of living it. The book introduces the armies and individuals, the events leading up to the battle, and the action on a day-by-day, moment-by-moment basis. Using scenes that show the interactions of some of the men involved, you see the problems faced and decisions made, as well as the personal and individual reactions to those decisions. Aside from these surface things, the book also conveys the reality of war, with its losses and tragedies, and the motivations and deep emotions of the men there.

A Brief Synopsis

The book starts with a Foreword that gives details of the armies and people involved. Four main chronological sections cover the days of Monday, June 29, 1863, through Friday, July 3, 1863, with the text alternating between the viewpoints of various Union and Confederate participants. An Afterword tells the reader what happens to several of the key characters. With the exception of the Foreword, which is written in the present tense, the entire book is written in the third person, past tense.

Each chapter within a section is from a different person's viewpoint, though the overall viewpoint of the novel is omniscient. Even though a chapter is written from one commander's perspective, the author still allows you to see what some of the other characters in those scenes are thinking. Also, you are able to watch that particular commander from outside himself as a spectator would.

The omniscient viewpoint gives the author a way to communicate many details, something that would be difficult to do through the eyes of only one person. This approach also allows for a broader perspective to the whole story because you see it through the eyes of so many people. The changing viewpoints and locations make it an active structure, which serves to intensify the emotions of the reader.

Shaara selects four main people as the viewpoint characters and moves back and forth among them to progress the story. This approach builds tension and allows personal connections to be made with the characters. Their backgrounds, desires, beliefs, and fears are revealed, and you see how these things, set against the canvas of events, will affect decisions and actions in the story.

On the Confederate side he focuses on Lee and Longstreet, while on the Union side he focuses on Buford and Chamberlain. He adds a couple of additional viewpoints to round out the story, using the characters of Harrison, a Confederate spy, Armistead, one of the Confederate commanders under Pickett, and Fremantle, an English observer on the Confederate side.

The viewpoint characters selected have significance for a few reasons. First, they give the reader a view of the action from the different levels of command. Secondly, they let you see the battle from two different locations: the sidelines and the action. Shaara's alternating of character viewpoints and locations provides glimpses of the planning, reasoning, and strategy sessions, as well as the in-the-moment battle experiences.

List of Characters

Confederacy

Lee, General Robert E. (the Old Gray Fox) commander of the Army of Northern Virginia

Longstreet, Lieutenant General James (Pete, Old Peter, Dutch, Old Pete, War Horse) 1st Army Corps commander and Lee's most valued commander

Armistead, Brigadier General Lewis A. (Lo, Lothario) Pickett's brigade commander, who was close friends with General Hancock before the war

Pickett, Major General George E. Longstreet's division commander

Garnett, Brigadier General Richard Brooke Pickett's brigade commander who was seeking to salvage his honor from an unfounded slur by General Stonewall Jackson

Early, Major General Jubal Ewell's division commander

Ewell, Lieutenant General Richard S. (Old Baldy) 2nd Army Corps

Stuart, Major General James Ewell Brown (J.E.B.) Cavalry Division commander who was controversial and flamboyant

Heth, Major General Henry (Harry) Hill's division commander

Hill, Lieutenant General Ambrose Powell 3rd Army Corps

Hood, Major General John Bell (Sam) Longstreet's division commander

Jackson, General Thomas J. (Stonewall, Old Thomas, Old Blue Light) forceful commander under Lee who was killed before Gettysburg and whose loss forced the reorganization of Lee's Army, placing several inexperienced generals in command positions

Pettigrew, Brigadier General James Johnston Heth's brigade commander

Kemper, Brigadier General James Pickett's brigade commander from Virginia who was speaker of the Virginia House and not fond of foreigners

Fremantle, Lieutenant Colonel Arthur Lyon Englishman of Her Majesty's Coldstream Guards, there to observe the Confederacy. His name is sometimes spelled Freemantle

Harrison Longstreet's spy

Pender, Major General William Dorsey Hill's division commander

Taylor, Major Walter Lee's aide

Trimble, Brigadier General Isaac division commander under Pender who led one of the groups in Pickett's charge; he was originally a volunteer under Ewell

Sorrel, Major G. Moxley Longstreet's chief of staff (sometimes spelled Sorrell)

Rodes, Major General Robert Ewell's division commander

Mary Armistead refers to Mary, in remembering the last night with Hancock and Hancock's wife Almira. While not specifically stated, it is assumed this is his deceased wife's name

Pickett, Sallie (LaSalle Corbelle) George Pickett's wife; at the time of Gettysburg she was his sweetheart

Union

Buford, Brigadier General John division commander in the cavalry who was the first to get to Gettysburg and was responsible for recognizing the good ground and holding it until reinforced

Chamberlain, Colonel Joshua Lawrence former professor from Bowdoin University who commanded the 20th Maine regiment that was primarily responsible for holding Little Round Top. He later was awarded the Congressional Medal of Honor for his bayonet charge against the enemy when out of ammunition

Chamberlain, Lieutenant Thomas Joshua Chamberlain's aide, and his younger brother

Kilrain, Former Sgt. Buster aide to Chamberlain, like a father to him

Hancock, Major General Winfield Scott II Corps commander; dynamic and brave, who on more than one occasion saved the battle

Meade, Major General George Gordon commander of the Union Army who received this command just before Gettysburg

Reynolds, Major General John F. I Corps commander; a fine commander killed the first day of battle

Rice, Colonel James M. commander of the 44th New York regiment in Vincent's brigade

Vincent, Colonel Strong Chamberlain's commander

Sickles, Major General Daniel (Bully Boy) III Corps commander who was infamous for killing Barton Key (Francis Scott Key's son) for having an affair with his wife

Doubleday, Major General Abner 3rd division commander in the I Corps who was replaced the amid reports he failed to manage his command well

Gibbon, Brigadier General John division commander in Hancock's II Corps who had three brothers fighting on the Confederate side, and had a reputation as a cold, icy man

Hazlett, Lieutenant Charles E. commander of Battery D, 5th U.S. Artillery in the V Corps, who reinforced Chamberlain and the other groups fighting on Little Round Top. He was killed shortly after arriving there

Hooker, Major General Joseph (Fighting Joe) commander of the Army of the Potomac until the night before Gettysburg when he was replaced by Meade

Howard, Major General Oliver O. XI Corps commander who outranked Hancock on the field but had to submit to Hancock's command on the first day of battle.

McClellan, General George B. commander of the Union Army, well liked by many of the troops, who was replaced for being too cautious

Warren, Brigadier General Gouverneur, K. member of Meade's command staff who was responsible for getting Vincent's men onto Little Round Top minutes before the Confederates tried to take possession of it

Weed, Brigadier General Stephen H. commander of a brigade in V Corps that reinforced the men fighting for Little Round Top

Character Map

Army of the Potomac

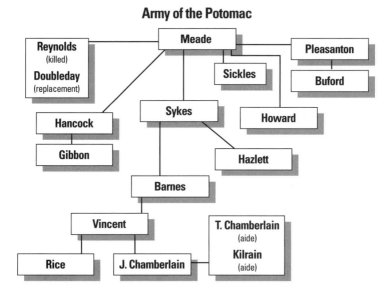

Meade

Reynolds (killed)
Doubleday (replacement)

Pleasanton

Sickles

Buford

Sykes

Howard

Hancock

Gibbon

Hazlett

Barnes

Vincent

T. Chamberlain (aide)
Kilrain (aide)

Rice

J. Chamberlain

The Army of Northern Virgina

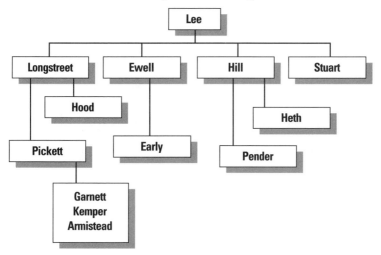

Lee

Longstreet

Ewell

Hill

Stuart

Hood

Heth

Pickett

Early

Pender

Garnett
Kemper
Armistead

CRITICAL COMMENTARIES

FOREWORD

Summary

The book opens with a present tense narration that sets the time, players, and place. It is mid-June of 1863. The Army of Northern Virginia is heading north behind the Blue Ridge Mountains, stealthily making its way to Pennsylvania. The Army of the Potomac is also moving, but slower, a characteristic that has plagued it for a long time.

The opposing armies are described, with information on their size, cultural makeup, beliefs, morale, and objectives. Major leaders are introduced, including Robert E. Lee, James Longstreet, George Meade, and Winfield Scott Hancock. Also, the setting is portrayed: hot rainy weather; men feasting on ripening cherries as they march and then suffering the after-effects of this diet; and areas deserted by the local population who suspect the coming conflict.

Commentary

Shaara's style is to the point here, placing the reader clearly in the location and time of the story — right before one of the major battles of the Civil War. His use of the present tense, while differing from the rest of the novel, gives a sense of immediacy to the situation. It is like listening to a newscaster report live on an unfolding crisis.

The descriptions of the major leaders are like a news exposé. Using details from their professional backgrounds and bits of gossip from their private lives, Shaara works to build drama and create interest in the characters.

Style & Language

The description of the armies reveals their qualities, motivations, and stark differences. The Confederate Army is a united group. The men in it have similar backgrounds, religious beliefs, customs, and language. While they are mostly unpaid, many cannot read or write, and their physical situation is difficult at best — no shoes, worn uniforms, and not enough food — their morale is very high. This is due in no small part to their unified belief in what they are fighting for — disunity with the Union — and their faith in their leader. They view

Robert E. Lee with the same reverence they have for their God, and they will follow Lee anywhere.

The Union Army is the opposite. They are a conglomeration of very un-unified men fighting for the unity of their country. They come from all walks of life, with different languages, nationalities, religions, and customs. They have seen mostly defeat, their morale is terrible, and they have no faith in their leadership, which changes often. Many are there for their own personal reasons.

Literary Device

One can feel in this introduction the increasing frustration in the ranks, and the desire for a definitive and final showdown. The two sides differ greatly in their makeup and morale, but one thing they both agree on: they want to settle things once and for all, right here and now, and go home. Without being told directly, the reader is aware that something powerful, ominous, and fateful is about to happen.

Monday, June 29, 1863

1. The Spy

Summary

Harrison is a spy hired by General Longstreet. Working behind enemy lines, he discovers important changes in the location, strength, and leadership of the Union Army. He has identified some of the units and determined where they are going and how fast they are moving. Though it is raining and almost dark, a dangerous way to approach a Confederate camp with its sentries, he does so anyway, feeling the message cannot wait.

Harrison's reception is marked by suspicion and disdain, as various Confederate officers question the validity of the spy and his information. Even Longstreet struggles with whether to trust him. The deciding factors are the nature of the news he brings and the lack of any concrete information from General J.E.B. Stuart. Stuart is supposed to be the Confederate Army's eyes and ears, but he has failed to contact Lee for several days. In Stuart's absence, Longstreet has no choice but to take a chance that Harrison is telling the truth. He brings Harrison to see General Lee.

Harrison gives his information to Lee and is then dismissed. Lee and Longstreet privately discuss what they have learned, Stuart's lengthy absence, and the implications of Meade as the new Union commander. Lee, though concerned about moving "on the word of a paid spy," orders the army to Gettysburg and the ultimate showdown with the Union Army.

Commentary

Several things are established in this first chapter: the prevailing attitudes in Southern society, character personalities and relationships, major story conflicts, and the style and strength of Shaara's writing.

The major ruling attitudes in the South are gentility, nobility, and honor. The commanders behave as gentlemen, and one's honor is more important than one's life. Battle is a means to glory in the South; it is

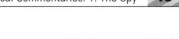

executed with the same nobility, romance, and excitement as with the knights of old.

In this society, Harrison is a despised man. He is a spy and in the knightly company of Lee and his men, spies have no honor. Even worse, he is an actor, another calling looked down upon. Harrison is portrayed unfavorably, with Shaara using such imagery as "The spy slithered down from the horse . . . grinning foolishly."

Harrison is also a man of conflicts. On the one hand, he has risked his life to come through the Confederate lines at night to bring vital information. And he vehemently states he is a patriot and refers to himself as a "scout," not a spy. On the other hand, his thoughts and actions throughout the chapter show he is a very proud man. He boasts about the way he does his work — it is a dramatic performance as he points out to Longstreet — and he only wishes he had an audience to witness it. It is not clear if Harrison is truly a patriot, but it is clear he wants people to see how good he is. He repeatedly reminds Longstreet of how good his information is, and Harrison takes great delight in revealing each tidbit.

Lee and most of his commanders show reactions ranging from discomfort to outright disdain. Even Longstreet approaches Harrison and his information with caution. Harrison's behavior and his treatment by Lee and the other officers shows the Southern code of honor in action. Gentlemen treat each other with honor and all others with disdain.

Literary Device

However, Shaara does foreshadow the demise of this code with some irony. Whatever Harrison's motivations, he has risked his life to deliver solid, accurate, needed information. There is no escaping that Harrison has done a brave job and done it well. Stuart, on the other hand, is supposed to be one of Lee's most favored, noble, and exalted commanders, but he has failed miserably. The biggest irony is that the best and only information on Union movements comes not from the aristocratic Stuart, but from the despised Harrison.

Character Insight

Lee is the ultimate honorable man — he does not smoke, drink, chase women, or gamble, and he believes totally in God. He is soft-spoken, always in control, and chooses his words carefully. His operating style is apparent — he is a decisive man who analyzes the information available, makes his choices, and then leaves the rest to God and his commanders.

He is opposed to the idea of defensive warfare, preferring instead the Napoleonic tactics of great armies marching toward each other for battle on the open field. Hiding behind defensive works waiting for the enemy to attack and using such things as paid spies are distasteful and violate his values. These themes influence his decisions throughout the book.

His choices have a streak of the daring, and it has made him successful against a foe with more money and supplies. Because he cannot afford to trade the Union man for man, Lee knows time is of the essence. Each battle must take a heavy toll on his enemy, and Lee's strategies reflect that. Given the choice between a battle strategy of playing it safe or gambling with decent odds for the big win, Lee will almost always pick the latter. In a sense, that is his only choice.

Lastly, Lee is from Virginia, as are many of his commanders, and his allegiance to his home state is his deepest loyalty. To him, the South *is* Virginia and the only reason he is in the war on the Confederate side is because Virginia seceded.

Character Insight

Longstreet is not ruled by the emotions of nobility. But then he is also one of the few leaders not from Virginia. He is instead a professional soldier, and a pragmatic one. He does not overlook anything important and obvious just because the source, such as a paid spy, is disdainful. He does not relish using spies and is not sure what to expect of them. But the lack of good information can lose a battle. So Longstreet hires Harrison.

Longstreet is grim, silent, and unconvinced that their tactics are right. He differs strongly from Lee in his approach to warfare. He is one of the few men of his time who sees beyond the glory of chivalrous deeds, to recognize that machines and weaponry, not men, will determine battle outcomes. He does not want to be in the North and does not believe in offensive warfare "when the enemy outnumbered you and outgunned you and would come looking for you anyway if you waited somewhere on your own ground."

Longstreet is also suffering deep grief. Three of his children have died of fever within a week during the previous winter. His quiet moments are filled with thoughts of them, and their deaths have left him a pained and changed man.

Yet there is still a closeness, respect, and almost affection between Longstreet and Lee. Longstreet is Lee's right arm since Stonewall Jackson's death after Chancellorsville. Lee respects Longstreet's advice, trusts his leadership abilities, and treasures his company. He is Lee's "old war horse." Longstreet, in turn, would do almost anything for Lee.

Jeb Stuart, too, would do anything for Lee, but he is also a grandiose man who seems to be a glory-seeker. In spite of this, Lee has a fatherly affection for Stuart, respect for his abilities as a cavalry leader, and unwavering faith that Stuart will not fail him.

Longstreet does not share these feelings. Longstreet considers Stuart to be a joyrider who likes to see his name in the newspapers. Longstreet curses Stuart for leaving the Confederate Army in danger by not providing needed information and protection.

One of the recurring questions throughout the story — "Where is Stuart?" — surfaces in this chapter. Stuart's absence for over a week is one that will influence almost every decision made by Lee and those of some of his commanders because without his reconnaissance, the Confederate commanders do not know what they are up against. This lack of knowledge will have a direct impact on the outcome of the battle.

Shaara's writing really powers the story. Well-chosen character details, creative descriptions, unusual similes, and strong active verbs, are some of the tools he uses.

To reveal Harrison's personality and previous career as an actor, Shaara has him quoting Shakespeare and using grandiose and theatrical mannerisms. Shaara shows Harrison's pride in his work when he has Harrison elaborate for Longstreet the various "performances" he does with the local people in order to obtain information. Harrison's murky values and past are further implied when Harrison reveals his name is just a small joke on the name of an ex-President and ex-General. No one knows who Harrison is or what he really stands for.

Powerful similes are evident throughout the story. On the first page of this chapter, the size, shape, and ominous nature of the gathering Union Army is characterized this way: "It . . . overflowed the narrow valley road, coiling along a stream . . . choking at a white bridge . . . like a great chopped bristly snake." He goes on to show that the threat is still increasing with the passage "the pressure of that great blue army . . . building like water behind a cracking dam."

Shaara creates sharp, clear images with his descriptions: "liquid Southern voice," "bleak hawkish grinning face," and "black diamond eyes." And action is portrayed forcefully and sensually with strong verbs: "He smelled out the shape of Lee's army . . ."

Glossary

(Here and in the following chapters, difficult words and phrases, as well as allusions and historical references, are explained.)

guidons small flags or pennants carried by cavalry guides. A guidon aided in identifying units and keeping control of the situation. It also was an emotional emblem inspiring the unit to defend it bravely, and the opponent to capture it.

Black Hats of the Iron Brigade refers to men of a Union brigade famed even among the Confederates for their courage as well as for the hats they wore — black slouch hats instead of the flat, visored kepis. The name Iron Brigade supposedly came from their performance during the battle at South Mountain where they stood and fought without wavering.

South Mountain in September of 1862, General McClellan's troops fought their way through three mountain passes on their way to a victory against Lee at Sharpsburg.

Vicksburg Early settler city in west Mississippi that was besieged by General Grant in the Civil War, just before the battle of Gettysburg. Jefferson Davis suggested that Lee secure Vicksburg first before heading north. Lee convinced him otherwise. Vicksburg surrendered to Union forces on July 4th, the day after the Confederate loss at Gettysburg. It resulted in the loss of the Mississippi River and divided the South in half.

Monday, June 29, 1863
2. Chamberlain

Summary

Shaara introduces Colonel Joshua Lawrence Chamberlain, commander of the 20th Maine Regiment. He is suffering from heatstroke after marching 80 miles in four days. Also introduced are his younger brother Tom, who is his aide, and Buster Kilrain.

Tom adores his older brother and struggles to remember to refer to him as a commanding officer when in front of the men. Kilrain is a career army man and former sergeant who was demoted to private after striking an officer in a drunken fight. Kilrain is the best soldier in the outfit due to his years of experience and, in spite of being demoted, he is Chamberlain's most trusted advisor. He is like a father to Chamberlain, and there is a deep affection between the two men.

At the start of the chapter, a captain from the 118th Pennsylvania delivers 120 mutineers to Chamberlain, with orders to shoot any man who won't fight. The mutineers mistakenly signed up for three-year enlistments when the rest of old 2nd Maine regiment only signed up for two years. Since the rest of the regiment has gone home, they want to be discharged rather than fight another year with any other regiment.

They have been starved, driven to exhaustion, and otherwise badly treated. The captain delivering them is disdainful of all Maine men, including Chamberlain who is a superior officer. Chamberlain confronts him with silent power that demands respect, and the captain, catching himself, snaps to attention and salutes Chamberlain. Chamberlain's handling of the Pennsylvania man is not lost on the mutineers, who have been watching the interchange closely.

When the unit is ordered to move out a short time later, Chamberlain speaks to the mutineers, letting the words come from his heart. He won't shoot them, knowing they have already done their share of fighting, and so he talks instead about his reasons for being there — the right of each man to become something on his own, his right to dignity and freedom. Chamberlain asks for their help and promises to look into their cause after the upcoming battle. As they march toward Gettysburg, Chamberlain is amazed and gratified to learn that 114 of the 120 men have decided to join his regiment.

Commentary

Chamberlain is not "regular army," but a former college professor. He is used to dealing with irritable, unruly students who question things, and he is used to discussing things to bring about an agreement, rather than threatening to "shoot" someone into compliance. His "professor's mind" questions things instead of accepting military dogma. He thinks deeply on the meaning of life and man, and he has a basic humanitarian and fatherly approach to dealing with his men. He cares for their needs and then *leads* them.

His basic humanity toward others is what ultimately reaches the mutineers and convinces them to join the 20th Maine. They have been fed, heard, spoken to kindly, respected for what they've already done in the war, and they are not going to be shot if they don't fight. They are willing to take a chance following Chamberlain.

Also, Chamberlain is a Maine man. The importance of allegiance to your home state first above everything is shown in the interchanges about "Maine men." You see the interstate rivalry and inter-unit disdain when the Pennsylvania captain who delivers the mutineers treats all Maine men with disgust.

The importance of Chamberlain's convincing the mutineers to join his regiment will be seen later as the battle at Gettysburg unfolds.

Glossary

flankers soldiers detailed to protect the sides of a marching column.

advance guards detachments of troops sent ahead to inspect and protect the line of march.

Huguenots Protestants in France in the 1500s and 1600s who were persecuted and massacred for their faith, by the Catholics.

road guards advance troops sent ahead of a military unit to detect enemy forces and protect the main force as it moves ahead.

skirmishers scouts who provided information on enemy strength and location, geography of the land ahead, and also screened the movements of the main force from enemy detection.

impressed seamen American seamen taken by the British from American ships on the high seas and pressed into service of the British Navy. The British claimed they were deserters. This practice led to the War of 1812.

Casey's Manual of Infantry Tactics an 800-page book of infantry tactics written by Union General Silas Casey and accepted as the official Union Army manual in 1862.

sound the General most of the actions of a military unit, from getting up in the morning, to going to sleep at night, were communicated by bugle calls. The General was most likely the call used by Chamberlain's regiment to notify the men to assemble and start their march.

Monday, June 29, 1863
3. Buford

Summary

Shaara temporarily shifts the point of view to the book's "narrator" to set the scene. The narrator describes the land west of Gettysburg and reveals that the Rebels are entering Gettysburg from the west, blue cavalry is approaching from the south, and the two are watching each other from across the fields in between. At this point, things shift to John Buford's perspective.

Buford is a Union general leading two brigades of cavalry that are ahead of the main army, looking for the Rebels. Peering through binoculars, Buford identifies the units as Confederate infantry and disgustedly notes that they are "gentlemen," when one of the Rebel officers waves his plumed hat at Buford.

Buford also notes the lack of Confederate cavalry, meaning that the Rebels have no "eyes" to find out what's around them. He understands the significance of this, senses there is power behind the units he is seeing, and instinctively understands what is shaping up here. In his gut, he knows Lee is here and the size of the battle that is coming.

Quickly assessing the local geography, Buford identifies the hills around a cemetery as "good ground" to be held at all costs. He knows if this ground is captured, many Union soldiers will die a bloody death, and the battle will be lost.

Buford sends scouts to collect information on what Confederate units are there, how many men, and who else is en route. He then sends messages to Meade and Reynolds asking for immediate help, though he is cynical that the help will come in time, if ever.

He places his men on the ridges west of town and makes his headquarters in a seminary nearby. This plan will allow the Union cavalry to stall any Rebel advance and buy time for the Union infantry to arrive and keep the good ground. If they arrive.

Commentary

Buford is an experienced soldier who has served out West. He has learned much from the Indians about guerilla warfare and doesn't place much emphasis on the glorious cavalry charges and other noble practices popular at that time. He is concerned with preserving the men of his unit and keeping the advantage of high ground for his army. Buford also has the vision to assess the situation and instinctively know what needs to happen to win. He is good at what he does, and just does it.

Buford doesn't like Union leadership and prefers the openness and freedom of the Wyoming snows to being this close to desk generals. He is bitter that at Thorofare Gap he and 3,000 men held out against Longstreet's 25,000 for six hours, waiting for help that never came. He has little faith in the Union generals and fears that help will not come in time.

Buford's disdain toward Southern society is obvious. He is no fan of courtly society or knightly warfare. His western army experience makes him a pragmatic commander interested in using the best and correct tactics for a situation, not ones designed for glory and honor.

Theme

The topic of good ground comes up again and again, and it is important to both the Union and to Lee. The owner of the high ground has the advantage, and that advantage can mean the difference between victory and loss, life and death. In the novel, Shaara shows Buford wanting this ground at all costs. This desire may not have been as strong an issue in reality. Buford did want the good ground if the Union decided to fight there. However, Gettysburg was not the only good ground in the area on which to fight. Meade had already selected an area near Pipe Creek as a possible alternative for battle. If the Confederates had captured the high ground at Gettysburg, it is likely that Meade never would have engaged them there.

Literary Device

The image of the white angel surfaces again later as the story and battle progresses. For now, Buford notices the white angel statue in the cemetery, with its arms reaching up to heaven. Near the end of the battle, Shaara shows us this angel again and what has happened to it. It is a symbol for the level of destruction to come.

Glossary

dragoon pistols pistols in use in the 1700-1800s that were single-shot flintlock technology, thus very slow to operate.

repeating carbines this is not entirely accurate. Buford's men were armed with breechloading rifles, which were an improvement over muskets. Breechloaders were loaded behind the barrel instead of down the muzzle as muskets were. While they were single-shot rifles, they were faster to fire and thus gave Buford's men the ability to hold off superior numbers of infantry. Buford did not, however, have repeaters, which could fire several shells before reloading was necessary.

Indian Wars from the time this country was first colonized by Europeans in the 1600s until the late 1890s, there were intermittent wars waged against various Indian tribes. The goals were either to eliminate them from an area the settlers wanted to colonize or, later on, to relocate them further west. Buford most likely grew up during the wars against tribes in Florida and the Southeast during the 1830s. As an adult, he saw action in some of the later Indian wars out West, before the Civil War.

corn dodger a small cake of cornmeal, baked or fried hard

Murat charge Joachim Murat was one of Napoleon's military commanders who was described as having little intelligence and no sense of strategy. His only ability to distinguish himself in battle was by leading dashing cavalry charges, but even there, his mistakes would sometimes almost cost Napoleon victory.

Monday, June 29, 1863

4. Longstreet

Summary

It is night in Longstreet's camp, and all the officers are relaxing around the campfire playing poker. Longstreet is renowned at poker, but no longer plays since the death of his children. He prefers to sit off to the side, close enough to listen, far enough away to be left alone.

Through the antics, jokes, and discussions of the officers, Shaara introduces the annoying Sorrel, the sentimental and honorable Armistead, the sad Garnett, the irritable Kemper, and the flamboyant George Pickett. They tease Pickett about finishing last in his class at West Point, his cologne, and his girlfriend, Sallie, who is half his age. They argue with the British observer, Fremantle, about when the British are going to come in on the Confederate side and break the Yankee blockade.

As they bicker, Longstreet ponders a number of things. He is concerned about the lack of information on the enemy so he has sent Harrison, the spy, to gather information at Gettysburg, which is still 30 miles away. When Sorrel reveals that Hill's men encountered Union cavalry that day but brushed it off as local militia, Longstreet is further worried. He suspects the cavalry are not militia, and where the Union cavalry is, the infantry is not far behind. Longstreet is frustrated with Stuart's absence and with Lee for not sending out other cavalry to scout ahead.

He has several conversations with various men in his command through the course of the evening, and these reveal each man's personality, beliefs, and personal history. These meetings also reveal a lot about what Longstreet thinks and feels, and we get a clear picture of the man and his demons. He struggles with the pain he feels for his wife and their dead children, he struggles to control his drinking, and he considers the men in his command more a family than an army.

Back at the campfire, the discussions have become heated. The Southern officers are trying to get the European observers to understand the Cause. The Europeans think the war is about slavery. The Southerners try in frustration to explain it's about state's rights to govern themselves.

The chapter ends with Longstreet telling Pickett to look after the men, then chiding himself for being too motherly. Harrison returns with news of Union cavalry, not militia, being nearby. Longstreet tries to get word to Lee; however, Lee's aide doesn't think it's important enough to wake Lee.

The point of view shifts to the weather changing from falling stars to rain and Buford's pickets readying for dawn. There is the approach of figures moving toward a Union picket in the early morning mist and then a shot.

Commentary

Characterizations, personal relationships, the Cause, emotional attitudes, and beliefs make up the bulk of this chapter.

Character Insight

Longstreet is a deeply emotional man who is trying not to be. He tries not to care too much for his men, but is motherly. He tries not to think of his children and wife, but is overwhelmed with pain. He avoids taking a drink and playing cards with his men, but wants to do both. And he tries to be easy and open with Armistead but is jealous of Armistead's close friendship with Hancock.

He is a romantic. Seeing a falling star, he remembers counting stars at midnight in a pasture with a girl, wondering if she loved him. At the end of the chapter, the falling stars turn to rain, a reflection on Longstreet's life. The past held happiness, joy, life, and connection. The present is loneliness, alienation, death, responsibility, and pain. And all of this is coupled with Longstreet's opposition to fighting an offensive battle, and a gut sense that this whole invasion and approach is a deadly mistake. His sense of foreboding is strong.

The discussions with Armistead show a number of things, including Armistead's close friendship with Union General Hancock. So many of the opposing commanders served together for the Union before they became "us and them." Also, you get a clear picture of southern aristocracy and of being a Virginian. There is the depth that honor and chivalry affect actions and decisions and the Cause as being about state's rights to self-govern comes up, along with the Englishman's misconception that the war is really about slavery.

Literary Device

The issue of honor is further intensified in Garnett's plight. His honor has been stained by Stonewall Jackson when Jackson in an earlier battle, accused Garnett of cowardice. As Jackson died before Garnett could clear his name, that leaves Garnett in dishonor. Garnett's personal struggles to deal with the dead Jackson's accusations are foreboding. It is interesting to note how Jackson, even though already dead before this novel opens, plays such a strong role in this story. Whether it is things left over from his command or Lee and others reflecting on "if only Jackson were here," the ghost of Jackson hangs heavily over the people and the battle itself.

Glossary

Her Majesty's Coldstream Guards regiment that Fremantle serves in. They are the personal guards to the sovereign of the British realm.

s'il vous plait French expression meaning: if you please, if it pleases you.

Chapultepec fortress on a rocky hill near Mexico City: captured (Sept., 1847) in an American assault led by General Winfield Scott in the Mexican War.

Old Soldier's Disease intestinal distress and diarrhea caused by eating too much fresh fruit along the march; in this case it's fresh cherries. There's a reference to having to shoot from a squatting position.

Lothario nickname given to Lewis Armistead and meant as a joke. A "lothario" is someone whose chief interest is in seducing women. Armistead is a quiet widower, a gentleman, and about as far from a lothario as one can get.

Black Watch 42nd or Royal Highland Regiment of the British Army, made up of Scottish infantry that wore its traditional dark-colored garb including kilts, which is where it got its name. It distinguished itself in the French and Indian War and the Napoleonic War, and apparently fought the United States during the War of 1812.

Lee's Miserables/Les Miserables Lee's Miserables is the joking name Armistead gives to their Confederate group. It is a pun on the name of the fiction classic, *Les Miserables* (The Miserable Ones), written by French writer Victor Hugo and published in 1862. The book chronicled the life of Jean Valjean, a victim of society who managed to perform heroic deeds in spite of the many unfair things done to him.

Scheiber a Prussian observer; the spelling of the name may be incorrect though, as most records indicate a Major Justus Scheibert as the Prussian observer.

old Richard and the rest a reference to Richard I of England, also called Richard the Lionhearted, and his soldiers in their unsuccessful Third Crusade.

Wednesday, July 1, 1863

1. Lee

Summary

In the early morning hours, Lee is struggling with chest pains and declining health. He has a strong sense of urgency in him to finish this war before his time, and that of the South, runs out. The attitudes of his men toward him show clearly. They view him with reverence and speak in hushed tones around him. Lee's aide, Taylor, comes through as arrogant and condescending, something Lee knows, but gracefully chooses to overlook.

There are momentary reflections of Jackson's death, and that others, such as Stuart, will die, too. Lee discusses the spy's news with Taylor, though Taylor airily discounts it. Lee decides to send a search party for Stuart if he does not show up by evening.

Taylor continues to update Lee on things: complaints from local people; Hill's lead division will go in to Gettysburg for shoes; Ewell is on his way; Hill discounts Pettigrew's claim that Union cavalry are at Gettysburg. Lee, though, questions this last one and knows that if Union infantry is coming, cavalry would be first. He repeats his orders with emphasis: The enemy is not to be engaged until his whole army is concentrated.

Lee meets with aides Marshall and Venable. Marshall wants to court-martial Stuart, and Venable wants Lee to speak to General Pender about a letter he received from his wife, who feels he will die as God's punishment for invading the North. Lee also meets with Longstreet to discuss strategy, and the two disagree on the course of action. Noting the foreign observers, Lee comments that there will be no help from those governments. They discuss their division leaders and disagree about what to do with the missing Stuart. Longstreet adds that his spy has confirmed the soldiers in Gettysburg are Union cavalry, not militia, something that disturbs Lee. Cavalry means Meade is coming, and fast. They are interrupted by the sounds of artillery. Lee rides off to see what's happening.

Commentary

You see firsthand Lee's heart problems and what he feels about his health. It is interesting to note that Shaara himself had heart problems.

Lee's basic gentleness and goodness show in how he treats his horse; his fairness in dealing with the local people's complaints; in his religiousness; in his concern about Stuart, and his faith that Stuart will not fail him. Lee's men react to those qualities with reverence, awe, and a willingness to do anything for him and excuse anything in him. Lee's gentleness even extends to irritating and condescending sorts, such as his aide, Walter Taylor.

The chapter also reveals the importance of the code of chivalry to many of the men of that time: Fremantle's eagerness for dashing saber battles and charges; Longstreet's mention of how Hill once challenged him to a duel; and Longstreet's observation that this is not an army but a gentleman's club.

Literary Device

The future is an element that comes up in this chapter. When Lee reflects on Stonewall Jackson's death, he also notes that they will all go, including Stuart, "like leaves from autumn trees." Lee is aware the war is coming at a high cost, and it will eventually claim all of them. Stuart will in fact be killed later in the war.

Shaara also does a more immediate foreshadowing of problems that will arise in this battle: Taylor's discounting of the spy's information on Union cavalry; Hill's belief that there is only militia; and Lee's concern that his new corps commanders, Hill and Ewell, will not live up to the standards Jackson set. Lee senses something coming and reinforces his orders not to engage the enemy. His unrest is dramatized when his heart beats irregularly as he learns more and more of what's happening ahead.

The letter from General Pender's wife shows concern over moral choices. She feels they are wrong to invade Pennsylvania and thus can no longer pray for her husband. Lee's aides also express their concern about the morality of the invasion, but Lee brushes it off with the thought "God protect us from our loving friends." He feels God's will and judgment will be made clear and that it is all in God's hands. However, even Lee ponders the fact that he's breaking the oath he took to protect the North, made when he was in the Union Army. He, too, struggles with the cloudiness of morality here.

With regards to morality and God, there is a touch of irony at the end of the chapter. Lee prays, "Blessed be the Lord my strength, which teacheth my fingers to fight and my hands to war." Lee believes deeply in God, a God who will even help him kill.

In the chapter, you glimpse Lee, the family man, and his personal relationships. He thinks of his wife — the tragic face of that frail, unhappy woman — and of his mother, with her stone strong face. He wishes the war would be over so that he can play with his grandchildren. The war is too late in his life for him to care about the fame. He would have enjoyed that more as a younger man.

Lee's relationship with Longstreet is portrayed more fully here. He takes joy in Longstreet's company, needs his support and strength, and depends on him. He notes Longstreet is not a "gentleman," and not a Virginian, but a strong steady, magnificent soldier, the rock of the army, and Lee is concerned for Longstreet's safety. This display of caring surprises but touches Longstreet, who is so in need of human emotion and fathering.

However, there are conflicts between the two men, and they come up whenever they discuss Jeb Stuart or battle strategy. Longstreet wants Stuart court-martialed. Lee feels docile men make bad soldiers and prefers to "reproach" Stuart instead. Longstreet correctly assesses that Lee could reproach Stuart and achieve results, but no one else could.

This shows Lee's power to manipulate his men because of their emotional connection to him as a father figure. Lee also understands that the kind of soldier he wants is one who rides the edge of the rulebook. Daring soldiers will sometimes err, but he needs that daring. So reproach rather than dismissal is the best tool in his mind. Lee is a psychological commander, motivating his men through their emotions, not the rulebook. However, there is no question Stuart pushes the limits and causes a fair amount of anger amongst the other officers. Even Lee's aides want to court-martial Stuart.

With regards to battle strategy, both Lee and Longstreet agree Union cavalry in Gettysburg means Meade is coming fast with infantry. And both know John Buford's reputation. Longstreet really wants to swing south around the Union Army and make the Union Army come to them. Lee is determined to fight here. Lee knows Longstreet's opinions about defensive warfare, wants Longstreet's honest answers, tolerates the differences of opinion, but will not yield in the final strategy decision. Lee will fight here.

Music is a strong theme throughout the book and starts to be noticed in this chapter. There are bands playing, giving an air of adventure as the Southern officers ride like plumed knights of old. The song, "Bonny Blue Flag," will appear again and again, usually in honor of Lee. The songs and their sentimental themes are a reminder of happier times, past friendships, and the splits between friends and brothers today.

Glossary

Maryland people refers to men under Confederate Major Harry Gilmore of Ewell's Corps (in this case, a group led by James D. Watters), who were from Maryland, knew the area, and were renowned for their raiding abilities in the area.

British/hollow square method of fighting off an attacking group by having the infantrymen form a square facing out on all sides with the officers in the center.

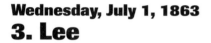

Wednesday, July 1, 1863
3. Lee

Summary

This chapter could be named "confusion, chaos, and frustration." Lee struggles to get a handle on what is happening at the head of his army, as well as get the army through a narrow pass before being attacked by the enemy. Lee senses his commanders may not be in control of things with their own groups. He is worried about bringing on a general engagement with the enemy before his whole army is in place. Shaking off his fear so as to think clearly, Lee prays for a moment and then goes on.

The confusion increases when Lee catches up with A.P. Hill, who appears to be sick, a usual state for him before a battle. Hill has little information on what's happening. Seeing Lee's frustration, Hill heads to the front to find out more. Lee waits for a bit, agitated about the current confusion and Stuart's continued absence. While bands play happy tunes, Lee fumes. Finally, he heads out to get his own answers.

The battle is bigger than he thought, and all his men are not in place. Longstreet and several other units are of no help as they're blocked behind the pass. Lee sends a message asking Ewell to hurry. Meanwhile, Harry Heth shows up and doesn't understand what is happening. Heth only grasps that he's created a problem against orders. Lee, realizing that Heth is beyond his limits, shifts his anger from Heth to the lack of information.

Things continue to change by the moment. Lee learns that some of Ewell's men are on the scene and preparing to attack the Union right. While this seems like a good opportunity to let Heth attack again on the Union left, Lee is not sure whether to proceed. Not knowing the strength of his enemy, Lee holds Heth back. However, when he hears of Reynolds' death and of the progress of Ewell's forces on the Union right, he changes his mind.

What follows is a rapid mix of chaos, confusion, and success. There is no clear news from Ewell as to how his men are doing, Hill is surprised at the resistance he is meeting, Heth is wounded, and Lee tells Hill to tend to himself and Heth. Things look bad, and then Pender's courier comes with news that the enemy is falling back.

But Lee also sees Union forces forming on Cemetery Hill, and he does not want them to keep the high ground. Lee orders artillery fire, orders Ewell to take Cemetery Hill if practicable, but warns Ewell not to take on a superior force.

Longstreet arrives, and the two discuss the events so far. Both agree things are almost perfect now, but this is where the conflict comes up. Lee feels this is the perfect place to battle the Union Army. Longstreet thinks it's the perfect chance to swing around the enemy and cut them off from Washington. In the midst of this discussion, Lee realizes that Ewell's men have not attacked Cemetery Hill yet, and his frustration mounts.

Longstreet leaves to check on his men, but not before Lee acknowledges that Longstreet's spy was right. Longstreet says nothing. Lee looks toward the battle, remembers how everyone called him the King of Spades at Richmond, and is determined to fight an offensive battle here.

Commentary

Character Insight

In this chapter, Shaara shows several things about Lee — how he manages fear and uncertainty, his faith in God, his belief in a divine plan that overrides his own plans, and his emotional self-control even when his commanders frustrate and anger him.

Lee is deeply religious and believes that while he is responsible for carrying out God's will, the actual outcome of the battle is up to God. Lee prays, makes his best decision, yet knows it was never really in his control anyway.

As a commander, Lee uses a nurturing approach with his men. While anger and fury flash through him regarding mistakes and broken orders, Lee tries to see things from his commanders' perspectives. He seeks out their positive points and works to strengthen those qualities instead of criticizing the shortcomings.

Yet as much as Lee loves his men, he also knows he will risk them all for the ultimate victory. His own son has been wounded and is in a hospital not far away. Lee will nurture and pray for his men, but he will spend them as he needs to.

Lee is a man of action. Instead of sitting around waiting for information to come to him, he gets on his horse and gets it himself. He is here to fight and win big for his side, and he is not going to do it meekly. He will confront and attack his enemy boldly, to the death.

He is also flexible in his planning, is an opportunist, and is daring and bold. Lee takes the problems and mistakes that come and alters his approach to meet the new set of conditions. If something goes against his strategy but appears to hold the opportunity of a bigger win, he changes his plans. This seems to contradict the image Shaara generally gives of Lee as being obsessed with only his point of view — to attack. It is Lee's constant revision of his plans to work around his commanders' errors that demonstrates Lee's flexibility in battle.

His command style is loose, and Lee likes to give his commanders room to carry out their orders without him micromanaging. However, his style may be too loose for a campaign this large and complex. The communications between Lee and his commanders are fragmented, incomplete, and verbal, the latter most likely due to his defeat at Sharpsburg. Verbal orders seem to be a problem here. Lee is not certain what his commanders are doing, they are not certain what they should be doing, and they don't know what their own men are doing. In addition, several of the commanders have broken orders about not engaging the enemy. Furthermore, when Lee's orders to Ewell to take Cemetery Hill "if practicable" but not take on a superior force, confusion reigns. It is almost not a surprise that Ewell doesn't attack.

Shaara also shows other themes here as well. The emotional connection between opposing commanders is seen in Lee's reaction to the death of the Union general, John Reynolds. Lee prays for Reynolds, mourns his loss, and reflects that Reynolds was a friend and a gentleman. It is not a war of strangers.

Good ground is another theme raised again. While most in the Confederate camp feel they have won a victory because the Union is falling back through Gettysburg, Lee notes that they are falling back to the high ground and digging in. He knows there is no victory yet, and he knows he needs that ground.

Lee and Longstreet agree the battle is going well, but differ on the next strategy. Longstreet favors a defensive move. Lee wants the offensive. Lee can't believe Longstreet would consider disengaging . . . retreating from the battlefield. Longstreet can't believe Lee doesn't see the opportunity in going around the Union Army. Their stalemate continues for the moment.

The element of chance and its role in this battle show up strongly: Heth's men go into Gettysburg seeking shoes and find Union cavalry. They attack again thinking there is only a tired brigade and find themselves up against a fresh division of Union infantry that arrived only moments before. Hill gets sick. Stuart is not around to give information on the enemy. Ewell needs help, but since no one is available or close enough yet, he cannot take Cemetery Hill. Circumstance is running the day.

Style & Language

Shaara's power of descriptions makes you part of the chaos and confusion of men running everywhere and commanders asking "What's happening?" You see the horror of war in the image of a horse's severed foot. You feel Lee's mounting anger and frustration.

In the midst of the chaos of thousands of men marching to fight, a band plays happy tunes. To the modern reader, it's seems strange. However, the bands boost morale, energize weary soldiers on a march, and inspire men before and sometimes during a battle.

Glossary

another Sharpsburg (also known as Antietam) in September 1862, Lee attempted his first invasion of the North, crossing the Potomac into Maryland. However, the Union Army intercepted his plans and passed them on to General McClellan. McClellan's troops fought their way through mountain passes and attacked Lee's forces near Sharpsburg. Though the attack was uncoordinated and piecemeal, the Union won because it had overwhelming superior in numbers. This reference in the chapter comes up when Lee is wondering whether Ewell's men, who are beginning an attack on the Union right, will end up victorious, or encounter large numbers of the enemy, as at Sharpsburg, and be defeated. Also, after this, Lee keeps his orders verbal to avoid interception. However, verbal orders only increased confusion in this complex battle.

Second Manassas all over again (also known as Second Bull Run) refers to the second Confederate victory in the Manassas area. On Aug. 29, 1862, Union General Pope attacked Lee's forces led by Stonewall Jackson. Pope was not aware Lee had split his forces and was surprised when he was attacked on his flank by Longstreet, who was leading the other half of Lee's forces. Pope was defeated. Lee had gone against standard military strategy when he split his forces in the presence of an enemy, but the bold move paid off.

Wednesday, July 1, 1863

4. Chamberlain

Summary

Chamberlain's group is moving west through the heat. Chamberlain is still sick from heat stroke, and though he wants to march with his men, Color Sergeant Tozier tells Chamberlain to get back on his horse and act like an officer. They don't want another new commander. Chamberlain is surprised by his men's looks of concern for him.

Bands play as they march. Tom Chamberlain and a man from the 2nd Maine discuss many things, including the unit's special bugle call, and how the smallpox inoculations kept the 20th Maine from fighting at Chancellorsville.

Chamberlain reflects on a number of things: the nature of marching itself, army life, the battle at Fredericksburg, winter in Maine, and home. He thinks of his mother who wanted him to be a preacher, and his stern father who showed so much pride when Chamberlain had given an oration at school on Man, the Killer Angel.

Colonel Strong Vincent, Chamberlain's brigade commander, comes by. Vincent tells Chamberlain about the new brigade colors, orders them to march through the night to Gettysburg, and relates rumors about the fighting that day. There is also a rumor that General McClellan is in charge again, something the men want desperately to believe. They finally reach Gettysburg about midnight.

Commentary

Character Insight

The main thing to note in this chapter is the further characterization of Chamberlain. He is an unusual man, a college professor turned regiment commander, and he views the war and the people around him much differently than a West Point graduate would. He is more a philosopher, and it shows in the things he thinks about.

Chamberlain ponders the army life; for all its inconvenience and discomforts, he loves it. He also thinks about the Battle of Fredericksburg, where his group was unable to retreat in the dark, pinned down near the stone wall all night, using dead bodies to shelter them from enemy fire.

He thinks of his father — the silent, hard-working, instinctive man — and remembers a conversation from his boyhood. Chamberlain told his father of a line from Shakespeare about man being an angel, and his father responded that man must be a murdering one. It inspired Chamberlain to deliver an oration at school on Man, the Killer Angel. His father was so proud, something he rarely showed, and Chamberlain wonders now how proud his father might be, given Chamberlain's current role in the war. He also reflects on "home," and that is home anywhere you are. Any one place is just dirt and rock. Home is within.

As they march and Chamberlain sees rows of dead Confederates from a battle when Stuart came through, he wonders, "Would the people here let the buzzards have them?" Chamberlain has a basic, unbiased concern for the welfare and rights of all individuals, not just Yankees.

He also cares for his men. Chamberlain took command of the 20th Maine from the previous commander, Ames, who was a tough man unconcerned about love. But Ames' advice stuck with Chamberlain: "You must care for your men's welfare. You must show physical courage." Chamberlain's approach toward his men, even the mutineers, is one of gentle nurturance for their basic needs. At the end of the chapter, he assesses his performance and decides that today he's cared for their welfare. Tomorrow he'd see about courage.A minor theme touched on in the chapter involves interactions within the Union Army. At the lower unit level, strong loyalty exists, as seen in the care Chamberlain's men show him. Toward the high-level leadership, a lack of trust dominates. And between individual units, much disdain exists. Respect for a fighting unit was not guaranteed because you were on the same side. The element of disease and how it ravaged troops shows up in the discussion about inoculations, and Shaara continues with strong descriptive elements, such as portraying a dead body in battle as "a wet leg of blood."

Glossary

Butterfield's Lullaby the bugle call written by General Dan Butterfield and meant for his unit. This tune later become known as "Taps."

Battle of Fredericksburg took place Dec. 12, 1862. Fredericksburg was a fiasco for the Union, which had to attack uphill. The Union soldiers spent the night pinned down under fire, incurring heavy losses.

Chancellorsville the battle took place on May 1 to 3, 1863. Lee's army, outnumbered 2 to 1, won a major victory over General Hooker and the Union Army. Lee, again, displayed his courage by flaunting military rules and splitting his army, not once, but twice as he manuevered around Hooker to defeat him.

Wednesday, July 1, 1863

5. Longstreet

Summary

On the evening of the first day, Longstreet rides over the battlefield on his way back to his camp on the Cashtown Road. His mood is gloomy, and his staff stays clear of him. He reflects on the deaths of his children and on what he sees around him — the coming disaster for the army.

Fremantle, the British observer, joins him. He is cheery and light and amuses Longstreet. Fremantle discusses Lee and what a noble gentleman he is. Longstreet talks of several things: how the army is a Christian Army, the theory of evolution, Stonewall Jackson and his eccentricities, how Jackson knew how to fight, and how A.P. Hill does, too.

Fremantle notes that Virginians are different than other Southerners. Honor is everything to Virginians. The two men speak of Garnett, and Fremantle just accepts without question that Garnett will die to restore his honor. Longstreet returns to camp where as long as there is a campfire there is company, and as long as there is company, he can banish thoughts of his children.

Commentary

Character
Insight

Shaara fleshes out Longstreet in greater detail through Longstreet's reaction to the battle and through his conversation with Fremantle. Longstreet's legendary black moods show up here, and his officers stay clear. Only the cheerful and oblivious Fremantle can break through the gloom.

Thoughts of his wife and his dead children break through, and Longstreet seeks the solace of campfire and company. He reflects on his dead son, on his wife who didn't even cry, and how he couldn't comfort her. It was the one strength he didn't have. The whole thing "pushed him out of his mind, insane, but no one knew it."

The Longstreet approaching Gettysburg is a much different man from the past, and he buries all his energy into his army. It is his only family now. His men are his boys, and Lee is his father. As to God, he didn't think God would do a thing like take his children. He doesn't believe there is a God listening out there.

Longstreet knows there is no talking Lee out of attacking the Union here. "Lee would attack in the morning . . . fixed and unturnable, a runaway horse." Longstreet smells disaster. It is his curse to see things clearly.

The themes of honor and of Virginians being special are also shown in this chapter. Fremantle sees traces of Englishmen in these Southerners, especially the Virginians, in spite of their earthiness and their crude habit of shaking hands. His thoughts on Lee show the attitudes of that aristocratic "gentlemen's" society: "Lee is a moralist, as are all true gentlemen. . . but he respects minor vice . . . in others." When Fremantle and Longstreet discuss the "new" theory of evolution, Fremantle's distaste shows through. He can't imagine a General Lee coming from an ape.

Honor also affects Garnett and his future actions. Disgraced by Jackson's accusations of cowardice and unable to clear his name because of Jackson's death, Garnett will most likely try to die in battle. This is the only way to restore his honor. Fremantle simply accepts it as the way things have to be. Longstreet argues in frustration that "the point of the war is not to show how brave you are and how you can die in a manly fashion, face to the enemy . . . it's easy to die." Longstreet feels a shrewd and defensive use of men and technology will win a war, and nothing is gained by honorable but wasteful deaths. However, in this group of Virginians and Englishmen, Longstreet's arguments fall on deaf ears.

In addition to being affected largely by honor, the Confederate Army is deeply religious. Fremantle notes that little whiskey can be found, and Longstreet confirms it is a mostly Christian army. Longstreet reflects on Jackson's religious fervor, noting he was a good Christian, and then ironically adds: "He knew how to hate." It is one of the many ironies of the war — Southern men fighting for their freedom but keeping slaves, devoutly Christian men killing with bloody and unforgiving zeal. It is the nature of this war.

Style &
Language

The author uses razor sharp imagery to give a clear picture of the horrors of war: "Mounds of limbs like masses of fat, white spiders." The mounds of limbs are the amputated legs and arms of injured soldiers. Medicine at that time could do little for injured men other than to cut off limbs. The butchery at Gettysburg resulted in large piles of these limbs everywhere.

Glossary

hollow square battle formation used at that time where several ranks of soldiers are lined up on each side of a square formation, and the officers and unit colors are in the center.

Solferino in 1859, during the Italian battle for independence from Austria, a major battle took place outside the town of Solferino between the Austrians and the allied French and Italian forces. The battle was fierce and involved a number of brave and daring charges by the allied forces. These resulted in heavy casualties but a victory for the allied forces.

Charge of the Light Brigade at Balaclava during the Crimean war in 1854, the British 13th Light Dragoons were ordered to charge the well-defended Russian artillery. In spite of the hopelessness of the situation, the brigade charged over a mile under heavy fire and was destroyed. Their courage and honor was immortalized in Tennyson's poem, "The Charge of the Light Brigade."

Wednesday, July 1, 1863
6. Lee

Summary

Lee heads north through town to see Ewell and find out why he did not attack Cemetery Hill that afternoon. In town, all of Lee's men are celebrating the day's "victory." With tears in their eyes, they watch him pass by.

Lee meets with Ewell, Early, and Rodes. He waits to hear what happened. Ewell is nervous, chatty, awkward. It is Early who supplies Lee with the condition of their forces and other details. Ewell defers to Early, something Lee does not miss. Rodes is silent as Early coolly states that they decided to wait for reinforcements and not take the hill. All agree the hill is now being reinforced as they speak and will be very hard to take. Lee feels Jackson's presence in the room, watching.

Ewell, led by Early, proposes that Longstreet handle the next major offensive, at the other end of the Union line. His forces have not been engaged. Longstreet could draw the enemy from Cemetery Hill, and then Early and Ewell can take it. Early derides Longstreet's defensive strategy of going south around the Union Army.

Lee reflects on Early, the man. Longstreet can't stand him. Lee ponders that, as well as their suggestions. His leaders have let him down. And the hill remains untaken. Lee leaves, pondering options. It is risky to withdraw so many men through the narrow mountain passes, and it is bad for morale to withdraw an army from the face of the enemy.

He returns to camp and dispatches one of Harry Gilmore's raiders, who is familiar with the Maryland area, to find Stuart and bring him back. He meets with an angry Trimble who feels Ewell botched it. Trimble emotionally asks for reassignment. Lee sends him off to rest for the time being.

Lee is worried and wants to see Longstreet, his War Horse, but Longstreet isn't around. Ewell comes by later, apologetic and eager to try again for Cemetery Hill. Lee is relieved, moved, nurturing. He sends the man off to rest and reflects on what losing a leg might do to a man's resolve to fight.

Lee's sleep is fitful because he is worried about Stuart and what to do. Saying a prayer, even for his dead opponent, Reynolds, Lee puts things out of his mind, leaves everything to God, and sleeps.

Commentary

Character Insight

Lee is frustrated with his leaders, but slow to comment or judge. He waits to hear their side and wants to give them every opportunity to succeed. He observes his commanders, their personalities, flaws, and strengths and reads the interactions between the men. He learns what makes his men tick so that he can use it to motivate them to the desired result — victory.

In spite of his frustration with Ewell, Lee reflects that Ewell is not a Jackson, and he can't be. He wonders if a man loses something when he loses a leg, even though a man's spirit is not in his leg or any other part. Yet Lee does not judge, acknowledging the wound has not happened to him and so he cannot understand. Instead, when Ewell returns later, apologetic and upbeat, looking to please Lee, Lee responds with nurturing and a recognition of what Ewell has managed to achieve. Lee lets Ewell know he realizes it's hard to be a new commander.

Lee's faith in God shows up, particularly at the end of the chapter. So much anxiety and so many questions crowd his mind. Yet he prays, turns it all over to God, and falls asleep.

The close relationships between enemy commanders are apparent as Lee thinks of the dead Union general, John Reynolds. He even prays for him. There is the respect for a worthy opponent, a fellow gentleman.

There is a glimpse of Lee's family relationships — his wife, "that troubled woman," and his wounded son.

The various personality conflicts of Lee's staff come through in this chapter. Early despises Longstreet and vice versa. Ewell is nervous and defers to Early. And none have the leadership skills of the legendary Jackson, whose loss continues to be felt as this battle progresses. His ghost haunts them.

Theme

The Lee/Longstreet strategy conflict comes up here. In a way, though Shaara is portraying Lee as obsessed with attacking, Longstreet is the dogmatic one. Longstreet has one strategy — take the defense. Lee continues to be confronted with problems, plans gone awry, commanders who don't fulfill missions, and he just keeps rolling with it. Lee takes what's there, not what he wishes for, and works with it. He rethinks it, makes new plans, looks for the new opportunity, and never loses faith. Lee is aware this battle may affect the outcome of the war. Longstreet shows no such creativity or flexibility.

Style & Language

Shaara's descriptive skills continue to be powerful: "Ewell had the look of a great-beaked hopping bird . . . his voice piped and squeaked like cracking eggshells . . . Ewell . . . was like a huge parrot, chortling." These words convey the image of an insecure commander more effectively than if Shaara just tells us that.

Wednesday, July 1, 1863
7. Buford

Summary

It is 2 a.m., and Buford rides along Cemetery Hill while the men continue to dig in. He is wounded, in pain, and looking for orders for what is left of his cavalry unit. At the farmhouse being used as a head-quarters, he encounters two majors arguing over who is in charge — Howard of the XI Corps or Hancock of the II Corps. Meade is not there yet.

Gibbon comes over to greet him. Buford learns that Howard's men were falling back during the battle, and Hancock came along and pulled things back together. Buford starts to head inside, but Gibbon stops him and briefs him on Howard's accusation that Buford's men didn't support Howard's right flank. Hancock joins them and is surprised to hear how involved Buford and his men were, something that leaves Buford feeling a bit better.

Meade shows up. Hancock and Meade discuss that this is very good ground, but Buford, who saved it, can't even get close enough to talk to him. Disgusted and tired, Buford has his orders and leaves.

Buford reflects on all the men in his company who are dead. The chapter ends with Buford talking to the dead Reynolds and noting that "we held the ground." Buford notes that the white angel that was in the cemetery before the battle is nowhere to be found.

Commentary

The theme of relationships in the war is touched on in this chapter. Gibbon is a Union general, but his brothers are fighting for the other side, a common theme for this war of brothers.

Most of the Union top brass are portrayed as ineffective. In addition, here is a battle that may determine the outcome of the war, and

Buford, who is weary to the bone, has to stand and listen to two majors argue about army protocol and which general is really in charge.

Literary Device

Shaara uses the loss of the white angel in the cemetery as a way to make the losses personal and real. At the beginning of the story, you meet the young lieutenants in Buford's command and see the white angel in the cemetery. By night, the lieutenants are dead, and the angel is gone.

Irony is evident when Buford, whose men managed to save the high ground, is accused by General Howard of not supporting Howard's flank. The reality is that Howard could not even hold his own ground, much less save the high ground, and General Hancock had to restore the Union lines during the battle because Howard could not.

Petty resentments show in Howard's jealousy of Hancock's leadership abilities and Hancock's popularity with the rank-and-file soldiers.

Thursday, July 2, 1863
1. Fremantle

Summary

It is 3 a.m., and Fremantle reflects on the coming battle and what an uncivilized hour it is for things to begin. Breakfast has an air of "seize the day," and Fremantle is anxious not to miss the battle today.

Fremantle observes the command meeting with Lee, Longstreet, and Hood. His emotions are high, and he feels a part of this group of "Americans," Americans who are really "Englishmen." He thinks much about the similarities and differences of Southerners and Englishmen, and Northerners and Englishmen. He feels the war is really about the South being like Europe and the North being different, and he concludes the great democratic experiment has failed.

Moxley, Longstreet, and Hood all indicate that the battle will be a bit later, although Longstreet really wants to wait as long as possible for Pickett to arrive. Fremantle rejoins the other Europeans to discuss Napoleon, theories of war, and women.

Commentary

Character Insight

Fremantle lives for the joy of battle, knightly honor, and daring exploits, as seen in this quote: "There was even an air of regret at the table, a sense of seize the day, as if these bright moments of good fellowship before battle were numbered, that the war would soon be over, and all this would end, and we would all go back to the duller pursuits of peace." He experiences a momentary sliver of reality when he sees Hood and realizes that he might not see him again alive. But the thought is lost amid the excitement of coming battle and visions of glory.

Fremantle's assessment of Southerners is that in spite of some odd and earthy quirks, they are Englishmen at heart. They tried the democratic experiment, realize it has failed, and will be back under the Queen soon. The slavery part he finds distasteful, but is certain they will dispose of that soon enough. The Southerners will be the victors in this war because they are Englishmen. In fact, Fremantle believes the cause of the war is that the South is like Europe, and the North is not.

Fremantle sees the North as this rabble of huge cities, many nationalities, and many religions. Their only aristocracy is wealth, they have no breeding, and they hate the "Old Country." But Southerners — they *are* the Old Country. His theory takes a blow when he thinks Longstreet is English and finds out Longstreet's really Dutch from New Jersey. But Fremantle shrugs it off. After all, Longstreet's not a Virginian, and even Fremantle senses that to most of the men in camp, the South is Virginia.

The Southerners' attitude toward the North shows up in the breakfast discussion laced with disdain for the Yankees, and the sarcastic response to Fremantle's question about why there are no defenses in case Meade attacks. It also shows in Fremantle's assessment of how the North is different from the South. Aside from Lee and Longstreet, who have a respect for some of the men they will fight because they commanded some of them, most of the Southerners feel nothing but contempt for the Union Army.

The elements of music and the rebel yell surface again. The bands in camp play lively polkas to rouse the men for the fight, then switch to marches as the battle begins. And Fremantle and Ross note the bone-chilling rebel yell and speculate if it came from the Indians.

Glossary

C'est le sanglant appel de Mars a reference to the bloody, screaming call of battle, referring to Mars, the god of war in Roman mythology.

Napoleons and Parrots types of cannons.

theories of Jomini Swiss writer Antoine-Henri Jomini who was one of the three major war theorists that emerged after the French Revolution and Napoleonic wars.

Bloody George George III, King of England during the American Revolution.

Thursday, July 2, 1863

2. Chamberlain

Summary

In the morning, Chamberlain wanders through camp, judging his men's readiness and generally lost in thought. He remembers dreaming of his wife, of her coming to him in her scarlet robe. "Away from her you loved her more. The only need was her." He recalls her misspelling of the word "dreamyly" in her letters.

While encamped, Chamberlain's men encounter some Southern prisoners as well as an escaped black slave. Tom Chamberlain talks with Southern prisoners and is confused to find out they aren't fighting for slavery.

The slave is wounded, shot by one of the local women in Gettysburg when he asked her for directions. Chamberlain and his men react to the black man with a mix of curiosity, strangeness, and revulsion, which is ironic given that they're fighting to free men like him. They fix him up and are surprised that he looks the same inside as a white man.

The slave cannot speak much English, but they determine he is thanking them and asking to go home, now that he is free. Since they don't know how to send him home, they bind him up, give him food, and leave him behind as they have been ordered to move out. They will see no action this morning, but are being held in reserve.

They march close to Gettysburg with thousands of other soldiers and then find a spot to sit and rest since they're not needed. Everything is quiet except for a message from Meade to be ready to fight as the enemy is there and that they will be punished by death if they don't fight. Chamberlain reflects on the foolishness of threatening a man at a time like this.

Kilrain notes that the black man is still following them and wants to offer him a rifle. He realizes there is little hope the man will ever see "home" again.

Kilrain and Chamberlain discuss black men, the nature of man, why they are fighting, the aristocracy, and "divine spark." Chamberlain relates the story of the Southern preacher and professor who visited Chamberlain's Maine home and spoke of the black man as if he was an animal. Chamberlain tried to make them see how wrong they were, but the professor asked him, "What if it is you who are wrong?" Chamberlain ponders this, decides he is not, then notices the smell of death drifting down to them. He waits.

Commentary

Character Insight

Chamberlain's reflections as he walks through camp show the changes in him as a person. He is no longer a detached man living on a lonely New England mountain, but a member of the human race. He is not the preacher his mother wanted. He is a father to his men, and he loves it. When he reads the letter from Meade threatening death to any man who doesn't fight, Chamberlain is angry. He realizes you don't threaten men at a time like this, you *lead* them by example. Leading them — it's his calling.

Chamberlain's reaction to the sight of thousands of soldiers as they approach Gettysburg is one of excitement. The lines of blue, with flags waving, is breathtaking to him. His own family relationships seem a bit strange. He doesn't think of his children much, although he does think of his wife in her scarlet robe turning to love him. She is the only thing missing here. Otherwise, this life in this army is everything he wants.

However, with regard to his wife, he comments, "Away from her you loved her more." It is a curious comment that implies some level of friction. She loves the South, their courtly manners, the heat and Spanish moss, and men's willingness to duel. She liked being the professor's wife and was outraged when he went to war. So there is the implication of some discord, and in fact they did almost divorce several years later. However, they loved each other very much and managed to work things out, remaining married until her death.

Considering that the Northern men are there to fight slavery, their reactions to the wounded black slave are interesting. There is Bucklin, with his sarcasm and uncaring approach, who wonders how much reward money they'd get to return him. The men watch the black man with fascination, as if he were an animal they've never seen before. No one is sure how to treat him, speak to him, or even relate to him as a human being, and they are all surprised to find he looks the same inside as a white man.

His blackness puts them off, even Chamberlain, who is surprised by the revulsion he feels. Chamberlain feels ashamed of himself, but he didn't know the reaction was there. It is an eye-opener for him. It's one thing to live in world of ideas and ideals and have opinions, but another to live the reality of your beliefs.

Kilrain and Chamberlain discuss the nature of man. Chamberlain talks of every man being the same and having a divine spark. He talks of the visiting Southern minister, sitting there genteel with his tea but viewing his black slaves like his horses. "How can they look in the eyes of a man and make a slave of him and then quote the Bible?" Chamberlain wonders, and he struggles with the Southerner's question back to him, "What if it is you who are wrong?"

Kilrain is interesting. He views most men as not worth dirt, but yet he has the most human compassion for the black slave of any of them. Kilrain wants very much to be able to send the man home, and later, realizing he can't help the man, curses the gentlemen who brought the man here. When Kilrain sees that the black man has followed them near to the battle, he wants to give the man a rifle. In his eyes, it's the only decent thing to do for any human being — black or white — when they are near a battle. It is Kilrain, the despised castaway himself, who has the most innate sense of right and fairness for any man.

Kilrain also doesn't judge anyone as a group, just one man at a time. He doesn't believe in divine sparks, isn't fighting for grand ideals, and has little faith that most men, white or black, will amount to much. His fight is with the aristocracy. He's fighting for the right to prove himself based on what he does, not who his father was. His fight is with those gentlemen who look at you as if you were a cockroach.

On the opposite side, there is the issue of the Southern Cause that comes up in this chapter. Tom Chamberlain speaks to three prisoners expecting to hear they are fighting to keep slavery. Instead they kept saying they were fighting for their "rats." He finally realizes they are fighting for their "rights" but even they don't know *what* rights. Tom doesn't understand. This illustrates a basic misunderstanding people have regarding why the war is being fought in the first place.

Glossary

Enfields and Springfields the two most common muzzle-loading muskets used in the Civil War.

Dred Scott a black slave who sued for freedom because his owner had taken him to a territory where slavery was expressly forbidden. His case went all the way to the Supreme Court, who in 1857, ruled against him.

Provost Guards a group of soldiers similar in function to Military Police.

Thursday, July 2, 1863

3. Longstreet

Summary

Lee considers his next moves using the information his aides, Johnston and Clarke, have gained from scouting the Union positions during the night. The Union is dug in on Culp's and Cemetery Hills, there are men on Cemetery Ridge, but there are no men on the rocky hills to the south (Little and Big Round Tops).

Lee confers with Longstreet, who notices the "bright heat" in Lee's eyes and feels alarm. There is no doubt in Longstreet's mind that Lee will have them attack. Although Lee wants consensus among his commanders, he finally just orders Longstreet to attack.

Looking at the map, Lee, Longstreet, Hill, Hood, and McLaws plan the exact moves. They will use Early and Ewell's plan: Longstreet is to start with McLaws and Hood at the far right, move behind the enemy line and up Cemetery Ridge, one unit after the other in step fashion. At the same time, Ewell and Early will attack Cemetery Hill. Longstreet tries to stall for Pickett, but Lee won't let him. Longstreet asks for time for Law to arrive and to position men and artillery. Lee acquiesces, but is stressed. Hill looks sick again, and Hood suggests swinging to the right of the Round Tops to get the enemy from the rear, but Lee refuses. He does not want the force of the attack diluted.

The men move off to get ready. Longstreet is to be led into position by Johnston, and he tells Johnston to take as long as he needs but to be sure his men aren't seen. Johnston, however, only scouted the enemy's position. He doesn't know the roads. Longstreet snarls at the missing Stuart who should have been there with this information.

Lee and Longstreet ride together for a bit on the way to the front. Lee talks of the nature of command and tries to gently work Longstreet to his side. They talk about the old days and fighting in Mexico, about the men they will fight today — men who used to serve under them. Longstreet reflects that the men in blue are never really the enemy, and that he and Lee have broken an oath, a sacred vow to uphold the Union. Lee brushes it off, staying focused on today's plans.

An aide informs them of a Union signal team moving onto one of the Round Tops. Lee leaves Longstreet to do his work. Shortly afterward, Longstreet and Johnston discover that if they stay on this road, the enemy will see them. Johnston is devastated. Longstreet is furious with Stuart for leaving them blind. They have to double back to Willoughby Run and go another way. Longstreet worries that the men are already exhausted, and between this delay and the time it will take to arrange an echelon attack, it will be late in the day. He sends word to Lee, who is growing more anxious.

Finally reaching the front, Longstreet starts to place his men for the attack when McLaws informs him there are Union soldiers in the Peach Orchard, something they were not expecting. He sends word to Lee and posts scouts. Hood argues that given this new development, they must shift to the right and go behind the Round Tops. To do otherwise will mean a slaughter of his men. Hood begs Longstreet to change orders. Longstreet can't . . . he won't. He knows that by following Lee's plan, he is ordering Hood and his men to their deaths, but he does not change the plan.

The attack begins with Hood. Longstreet holds back the anxious McLaws until the right moment. Then he releases him and Barksdale, who runs off screaming, hair streaming like a white torch.

Commentary

Longstreet knows Lee has made up his mind. There is no hope, and at this point, Longstreet just wants to get it over. He gives up on whatever he believes, abdicating his responsibility to Lee's orders.

Both Lee and Longstreet have valid points of view, but the interesting thing is that if Longstreet had attacked earlier in the day, the Union Army wouldn't have been in the Peach Orchard or on the Round Tops. Because the Confederate attacks started so late, Union General Sickles had already moved his men forward, and General Warren had obtained Colonel Vincent's brigade to cover Little Round Top. On the flip side, there is no guarantee that the Confederates would have succeeded in an earlier attack if the enemy had seen them moving into position. It might have been a slaughter as the Union could have reinforced its lines in time. The element of chance comes into play here with timing, with no one knowing the roads, and with the missing Stuart, whose presence could have avoided some of the problems.

Character Insight

In this chapter, a lot is happening and being felt, but little is being said. There are shifting looks and a lot of "yes sirs." The personal interactions as this attack is planned and carried out reveal the characters and how they feel about one another. For example, Lee constantly checks up on Ewell, but not on Longstreet — a measure of his trust in Longstreet. When Lee mentions Early to Longstreet, Longstreet spits on the ground — a not so subtle expression of Longstreet's feelings for the man. Lee keeps trying for Longstreet's approval — really wants it — but he can't get it. And Longstreet wants to give it because he cares about Lee, but he just can't. A.P. Hill is sick again on the day of battle, a trend. And McLaws is caught between his commander's (Longstreet's) feelings about the battle plan, and those of Lee.

Later, Hood wants to go around the Round Tops, and Longstreet agrees that Hood is right, but he won't change Lee's orders. It's the impossible situation. Longstreet is sending his men to their deaths, to do the very things he disagrees with, and it's killing him. But he will no longer fight Lee. Longstreet just wants to get on with it. He reflects on the preciousness of his men and that they should be used carefully. He struggles with this and cannot even look Hood in the eye as he orders him to attack.

Lee also continues to manipulate Longstreet. He speaks again to Longstreet of his health, of getting older, of needing Longstreet, and of wanting total honesty from him. Lee says the things he knows will tug at Longstreet's emotions in the hope that Longstreet will agree with him. Lee needs Longstreet's friendship as much as Longstreet needs the father figure in Lee.

One of the problems with this battle is that Lee is executing very complex strategies, something that requires flawless, close, and constant communications and precise timing. Instead, because the communications here are verbal ones delivered by messengers, they are fragmented, ineffective, and confusing. Lengthy and costly delays result.

Theme

There is again the mention of the oath to defend the Union being broken. Longstreet feels it. Lee pushes it away. The higher duty to Virginia is Lee's guiding force, the indication that in that time, one's state came before anything else, even before an oath to God.

Longstreet recognizes that the men they are battling are old friends, not an "enemy." And he knows they will not be easy to take. He cannot shake the futility of this whole affair.

Glossary

en echelon an arrangement of units in a step-like manner to the right or left of the rear unit. When attacking, the first unit starts with the others coming in one by one in sequence, like a wave moving forward from one side to the other.

Ewell's people will demonstrate Ewell's forces will create a diversion on the left to keep the Union from reinforcing the line where Longstreet will be attacking.

enfilade fire fire directed at the entire length of an enemy line, such as when an attacker fires from the side of that line right into them.

the high Rocky Hill the name the Confederates were using for Little Round Top, as they did not know its name at the time.

vedettes mounted guards placed ahead of pickets, well ahead of an advancing force, to watch the enemy movements and notify commanders.

Thursday, July 2, 1863
4. Chamberlain

Summary

It is late afternoon. Artillery fire is heard in the west. Chamberlain and Kilrain are ordered to form the regiment and follow Vincent. The Confederates are moving on the left flank. Vincent explains how Sickles moved his men into the Peach Orchard against orders and that he has endangered the whole Union line.

Vincent places Chamberlain's men on Little Round Top, emphasizing that they are the end of the Union line and must hold at all costs. He leaves to place the rest of his brigade.

Chamberlain looks over his men and the terrain and then places them. He sends one unit far into the woods to alert him if the enemy tries to flank them. They can see the battle below in the Peach Orchard and that Sickles' units are being flanked.

Chamberlain convinces three of the six remaining mutineers to fight. The last three will have no part of it, and Chamberlain wastes no men to guard them. He merely says he expects them to be there when this is over.

The fighting starts shortly after their arrival. Men go down. The action is fast. Wave after wave of Confederate attacks are repelled, but the cost is high. Kilrain is wounded, but keeps fighting. Chamberlain notices a flanking movement, climbs up on a boulder to direct the defense, and is hit. But he continues to fight. To counter any more flanking moves by the enemy, Chamberlain orders his line to be stretched out and then near the end turned at right angles to the rest of the line. This way, any flanking movement will be met head on.

They continue to repel attacks, but are about out of ammunition. Men are falling dead all around him, and Chamberlain keeps shifting men, taking ammunition from wounded, trying to make every last man and every bit of supplies count. At one point, Chamberlain even uses his brother Tom to plug a hole in the line. Chamberlain reflects briefly on this, noting Tom is okay.

With a third of the men gone, the rest exhausted, the ammunition used up, and the awareness that they can't pull out no matter what, Chamberlain does the only thing left. He orders his men to fix bayonets and execute a right wheel forward. They charge down the hill, overwhelm the Rebels, and take hundreds of prisoners. This battle is over.

Amazed congratulations come in from the other Union commanders. The Union men are exhausted, exhilarated, and triumphant. Their casualties number almost half the regiment, about the same number they took on when Chamberlain convinced the 2nd Maine mutineers to join them. They realize they fought off four Southern regiments. Yet there is gentleness shown to the prisoners. Chamberlain spared a man at lance point during the charge, and later he shares water with the vanquished soldiers.

Kilrain is seriously wounded. He was shot a second time during the battle, yet prevented someone from shooting Chamberlain. The two men share an emotional moment as Chamberlain wordlessly acknowledges the pride in Kilrain's eyes. They try to minimize the seriousness of Kilrain's wound, but Chamberlain feels alarm seeing the weariness in the old man's eyes.

Chamberlain is ordered by Colonel Rice to move his men to cover Big Round Top. Rice is the new brigade commander as Colonel Vincent was mortally wounded during the battle. Chamberlain reflects that they are again the extreme flank of the Union line. He readies the men and then says good-bye to Kilrain, the man who had welcomed him to the regiment, the man who had always been there. Chamberlain does not know what to say him and moves away. Looking over the battle scene one last time, he feels incredible joy at their success.

Commentary

"Now we'll see how professors fight." This comment by Colonel Vincent alludes to the theme of Chamberlain's unusual background. He is not a politician, not a military man, but a professor. However, because he's not been trained to think like a West Pointer, he possesses the unique ability to objectively study situations and men, nurture and care for his regiment, see both sides of the fight, and do the unexpected.

It is these qualities that got the mutineers to join his group. Without his ability to influence people, the mutineers might not have joined the 20th Maine, and Chamberlain might not have had enough men to hold the flank. The entire Union line and the outcome of the battle were saved by the fact that he had enough men to do the job and that he could inspire those men to hold their positions. Chamberlain didn't have to threaten his men. He led them.

Character Insight

During battle, Chamberlain is calm, quiets the "talking" in his head, and just gets to work. In the middle of the fighting, he again shows that objective streak, noting that the men opposing him are very good. He feels strong emotions for Kilrain, like a son coming to the father to accept praise for a job well done. And he feels the loss when the man who has always been there is carried away. Lastly, Chamberlain experiences overwhelming joy when he reflects on what they've just done, and a sense of the importance of the moment.

Chamberlain struggles, however, with the morality of plugging the line with his brother. This issue has come up before and is now something Chamberlain needs to confront. He used his brother like a tool. He feels strong emotions for his brother, but must repress them, as he is first, a commander, second, a brother. This situation is not tolerable, though, and a change will have to take place.

Style & Language

Shaara's choice to have Chamberlain check on his men before the battle helps readers connect with these men on a personal level. You get to know the three mutineers who volunteer to fight, the Merrill brothers, Private Foss, and Amos Long. At the end of the chapter, you feel relief or loss as you learn who lived and who died. Shaara's descriptions put you right in the battle. You see the enemy approaching, feel the terror, and hear the bullets, rebel yells, and cries of pain. Shaara uses short sentences, quickly shifting scenes of the action, and vivid images of faces shot off, to create tension and reality.

Glossary

the Bully Boy nickname for Sickles given by other Union officers suggestive of his temperament.

the Barton Key Affair Barton Key, son of Frances Scott Key who wrote The National Anthem, was having an affair with Sickles' wife. Sickles killed him and then pleaded temporary insanity, the first time that defense was used, and was found not guilty.

the colors the flag for a particular fighting unit, such as a regimental flag.

red battle flags flags used for Confederate units.

brogans a heavy work shoe, fitting high on the ankle.

refuse the line to form a new line at an angle to the existing one so as to cover any flanking move.

right wheel forward like a swinging door, the line of men moves forward as if swinging from a hinge point in the main line, sweeping across the front of the battlefield.

mick slang term for an Irishman.

twicet twice.

shelter halves tarp halves used to make tents and shelters when setting up camp.

map error an error on the map shows the units on Little Round Top. The map shows the 118th PA on the top right. It was actually in the Wheat Field. The 16th Michigan was the unit next to the 44th NY on Little Round Top.

Thursday, July 2, 1863
5. Longstreet

Summary

Longstreet visits Hood in the hospital and lies to him about winning the battle and the number of casualties. Hood is drugged and about to have his arm operated on, so he is incoherent as he mumbles that Longstreet should have let him go to the right. Longstreet rides away, the rage building inside.

He sends his trusted Texas aide, T.J. Goree, to scout beyond the Confederate right. Longstreet does not want another countermarch in the morning like today. Longstreet learns Goree has been in a fight to defend Longstreet's good name, as Hood's men are blaming Longstreet for their loss. No one will blame Lee, and Longstreet knows it. He feels Lee needs to hear the truth, but even Longstreet is hesitant to blame Lee. Yet when he hears that Hood's losses that day were 50 percent, Longstreet feels Lee must know a major assault is out of the question.

General Pickett sends word that his group arrived earlier in the day and was told by Lee to rest. Pickett is concerned his Virginians will miss the fight.

Longstreet heads off to talk to Lee. Headquarters is a mass of activity: bands playing, men laughing, smells of whiskey and roasting meat, civilians in good clothes and sleek carriages coming to see how the army is doing. Foreign observer, Ross, is intoxicated. And there, by the fence, cavalier, lounging with a circle of admirers and reporters, is Jeb Stuart.

Longstreet avoids him. Stuart is Lee's problem. Longstreet tries to get through the crowd to Lee. The crowd hushes as Lee comes out. He is like a god to them all. Gentle Lee speaks first to Longstreet's horse, then raising a hand with no strength left, greets Longstreet. He shows fatherly concern and dissolves all of Longstreet's defenses. There is a commotion as Stuart joins them. Longstreet just wants to be out of there.

Lee's song, "Bonny Blue Flag," plays in the background. Finally Lee and Longstreet move inside, but it's crazy there, too. Lee clears them out, and the two men discuss the battle. Lee eyes are filled with visions of victory as he speaks: "It was very close . . . They almost broke. I could feel them breaking."

Longstreet, dumbfounded, is unable to argue with Lee. He tells Lee he lost half his strength that day and tries to get Lee to consider a move to the right. But Lee, focused on victory, puts him off. Longstreet, who's in a rage, leaves.

Lee's aide, Marshall, confronts Longstreet. The man is furious and has papers for Stuart's court-martial, but Lee won't sign. He confirms Stuart was joyriding and wants Longstreet speak to Lee. Longstreet agrees to talk to Lee and understands Marshall's anger. But he feels there is not much he can do about it.

Longstreet rides back to his camp with Fremantle. Fremantle praises Longstreet and Lee for the day's work and talks about what a clever and devious man Lee is and how you wouldn't expect it. Longstreet's smoldering rage explodes. He shoots that theory to shreds and lays out for Fremantle that Lee uses no clever tactics, it's just that the men love General Lee and will do anything for him. Lee moves quickly and boldly and often gets the good ground. He speaks of Chancellorsville, where Lee broke military rules by splitting his army twice. Realizing what he's just said, Longstreet excuses himself and rides off, alone with his thoughts.

Armistead comes by, encouraging Longstreet to join the rest by the campfire. Longstreet wants a drink, but declines. The two men talk about Garnett and why the English and Europeans aren't helping the South. Armistead fumes, but Longstreet says nothing. Slavery is not what Longstreet is fighting for, but in his mind he believes it is what the others are fighting for.

Their conversation is interrupted by singing in camp. The song is "Kathleen Mavourneen." Armistead is emotional and tells Longstreet that the night before he and Hancock went their separate ways to fight this war, they and their wives got together one last time. They sang that song. Armistead tells Longstreet he made an oath that night that if he should ever raise a hand against Hancock, may God strike him dead. Longstreet, already aware of broken oaths, shudders inside. Armistead tells Longstreet he sent Hancock's wife a package to be opened if he should die. Longstreet wants to reach out to Armistead, but cannot.

Weary of command, responsibilities, and emotional intensity, Longstreet agrees to join Armistead and the rest of the men for one drink by the campfire.

Commentary

Longstreet is becoming the scapegoat. Lee will never be blamed for any losses. "The Old Man is becoming untouchable." Armistead sums up the feelings for Lee when he tells Longstreet they don't need any help as long as Lee is there to lead them.

Even Longstreet cannot fight Lee. He melts when Lee nurtures him, and he feels protective when he sees Lee feeling weak. Longstreet knows Lee needs to hear the truth and is angry with himself when he does not speak it.

Longstreet is rough around the edges, and although he is an emotional man, he does not always express it well. For example, Longstreet notices that his aide, Moxley Sorrel, is wounded. Sorrel frequently irritates Longstreet, but Longstreet attempts concern: "Take care of yourself, Major. You aint the most likable man I ever met, but you sure are useful."

Longstreet struggles with emotion in general. He feels deeply for Armistead's suffering and wants to touch the man, comfort him. But Longstreet can't do it until they joke about hitting Early with a plate back in the old days. Then, with the emotional spell broken by a joke, Longstreet can lightly touch Armistead, once. Longstreet is in emotional pain, but can't let it show. The depression is deep — so many men dead, Hood's accusing eyes, his dead children — and Longstreet tries not to think about any of it. He stays away from his feelings.

Longstreet has been careful throughout the book to avoid any alcohol. He knows he is vulnerable already. However, after today, Longstreet wants to have a long sleep and a long bottle. He can't take the pain anymore. At end of the chapter, Longstreet doesn't want to be responsible anymore. He just wants to be with the men and let go. So he agrees to join Armistead and the others for one drink.

Shaara describes the condition of Lee's health through subtle references in the chapter: the hand with no strength; sitting inside — sagging, lines of pain around the eyes; saying he's tired, which he never did before; his hand going to his chest; his face gray and still. Lee is slipping away.

Theme

The theme of honor comes up several times in this chapter. Fremantle, so emotional over Longstreet's courage at being in the front line of battle, is actually willing to shake Longstreet's hand even though Fremantle hates that custom. Longstreet recalls Jackson ordering pikes — a weapon out of the dark ages of knights and castles — to use against the enemy if necessary. Longstreet can't believe the mindset and concludes they all come from another age, "The Age of Virginia." And Garnett, the unsmiling, dishonored, gallant man, will die in battle just to erase the stain on his name put there by Jackson.

Literary Device

Shaara chillingly foreshadows Armistead's fate when Armistead relates to Longstreet the vow he made to Hancock: "Win, so help me, if I ever lift a hand against you, may God strike me dead." Longstreet feels a cold shudder. Longstreet already feels the weight of other broken vows, being an invader on soil he had sworn to defend. This battle is the first time Armistead is up against Hancock, and while Armistead won't sit the fight out, he senses the vow may come to pass. So does Longstreet.

Music plays a large role in this chapter. Celebrations occur in camp after the battle, with happy music and partying. The Irish tenor singing "Kathleen Mavourneen" leaves the whole camp silent and many in tears. One lyric from that song — "It may be for years, and it may be forever" — continues to recur throughout the chapters in connection with Armistead, his memories of his dead wife, and his parting from his friend, Hancock. It symbolizes the ambiguousness of Armistead's situation — in his wife's case, she is gone forever; in Hancock's, it may be years before the two men see each other again, or it may be forever, if one or both die.

Glossary

sutler's store a sutler was a camp follower or merchant who was allowed by the army to sell provisions to the soldiers from his wagon, which was his store.

Thursday, July 2, 1863

6. Lee

Summary

Lee is working late into the night, sitting in a rocking chair to minimize the chest pain. The following day will be Independence Day, and Lee wonders if it is an omen for today's coming battle, a message from God. He doesn't even want to dream on the possibility of it being a Southern Independence Day.

Lee sits alone with his horse and ponders the choice of moving to better ground or staying here to fight to the end. He thinks about the choices he has made in his life. He struggles with what to do next. His thoughts are interrupted by Stuart's arrival.

Lee chastises Stuart with an icy voice, the father giving a hard lesson. He wants the spirit in the man saved, just reined in. Stuart responds with anger and insulted honor, offering to have a duel with the person questioning his actions and then offers to resign. Lee is hard and cuts him off, telling him there is no time for this display. But Lee is also melting. He feels pity as Stuart leaves and realizes Stuart will now be reckless to prove himself.

Venable, his aide, returns from visiting Ewell and reports that the camp is in confusion. Ewell couldn't get his corps into attack position until hours after Longstreet had started. Rodes never attacked, Early attacked at dusk, hours late, and then quit. Johnson managed to capture some trenches. Lee reflects on how Jackson would have handled this. He knows he can now only depend on Longstreet with Pickett's fresh Virginians.

Lee makes his most important decision quickly and doesn't think of the men who will die. He will attack with Longstreet and use Pickett's men to hit the middle of the Union line. It will be weak since the Union has reinforced the ends of its lines. He will send Stuart around to the rear of the Union line, to finish it off. With his plans made, Lee prays.

Commentary

Divine influence and power play a large role in Lee's life. In this chapter, Lee ponders whether God is sending an omen for battle since tomorrow is Independence Day. He makes his decisions after praying, knows the outcome is out of his hands, and releases it all to God.

Lee feels his only power is over men's spirits. He has manipulated his men throughout the book. He understands what makes his men tick. By providing what each man needs emotionally, Lee can draw out the response he needs for victory.

Lee's sole allegiance has always been Virginia and his decision to join the Confederacy stems from that. He fights, not for the land because land is not worth war, but for his people and family. In this regard, he is similar to Chamberlain, who feels that home is wherever you are, and people don't fight for dirt. They only fight for something that means something to them. But still, Lee is aware he's breaking an oath by invading the North. He knows he will pay in some way for that breach of honor, and he accepts that.

While Shaara portrays Lee as obsessed with only the option of staying to fight, Lee gives consideration to all possibilities here. This flexibility seems to contradict, at least somewhat, Shaara's portrayal of the man. He decides to stay and fight not out of narrow-mindedness, but because he has no guarantee of better ground elsewhere and because the effect on the men's morale to leave the enemy in control of the field would be bad. He realizes that their morale, pride, and emotions are their most potent weapons, and he cannot afford to damage that.

Stuart is like the adolescent who needs a stern father once in a while. He is angry at the questioning of his honor and wants revenge. Lee has the bigger picture in mind and basically tells Stuart to take it like a man and learn. At the same time, Lee knows Stuart will now be reckless to redeem himself. While he notes this is something to beware of, this recklessness is exactly the response Lee wants from Stuart. A crazed and furious Stuart will wreak havoc on the enemy tomorrow in his attempt to redeem himself in Lee's eyes.

1. Chamberlain

Summary

Chamberlain and his men have spent the night on Big Round Top. He has kept moving to keep the pain in his leg down. At dawn, Chamberlain climbs a tree on the crest where he can see the movements and campfires of both armies as they awaken. He smells coffee. But his camp has no coffee, no food, and no ammunition.

He has had men on guard all night. Joined by the 83rd Pennsylvania and the 44th New York, Chamberlain has changed the pickets every two hours and had them report to him every half hour.

He thinks of his wife again, and her red robe. He thinks of his children, how he was a teacher a year earlier, and how hard it will be to go back to normal life after yesterday's experience.

Tom joins him with some coffee taken off a dead soldier. They talk of the battle, of how proud Tom is of his older brother, of how good the attacking men were, and of winning the war. Tom mentions how he just couldn't use his bayonet on a man. He noticed that very few of the men could.

Cannons rumble on Cemetery Hill, and Chamberlain thinks it might be a diversion. He feels they can hold these rocks if they just have some food and ammunition. He sends Tom to alert the guards to be sharp and to send for ammunition. Chamberlain checks on his men, talks with them, and sends some of the wounded to the hospital.

He is starting to get anxious for food and supplies. Fatigue, pain, and hunger leave him feeling forgotten, unappreciated, and angry. Don't they know his men saved the whole line yesterday? His leg wound tears open, and he pulls off the boot wishing for something to clean the wound with. But the available water is dirty and bloody. Plum Run, the creek below is choked with yesterday's dead. He looks at his men and realizes they are almost gone. They started with 1,000 men. Now there are less 200. The Union Army fights a unit until it bleeds to death.

The battle at the north end of the ridge has increased in intensity. Finally, a courier from Rice tells Chamberlain and his men that Colonel Fisher's people will take over. Chamberlain doesn't want to go, but he gets the men ready. A lieutenant leads them to their new position to rest . . . right in the center of the Union line.

Commentary

Character Insight

This chapter gives more insight into Chamberlain's relationships with his wife, brother, and Buster Kilrain. Again, while Chamberlain misses his wife, he doesn't seem overly upset to be away from her and his children. The situation with Chamberlain's brother is requiring a resolution. And he feels the loss of Buster Kilrain, the man Chamberlain wants to talk to after a battle.

Chamberlain experiences a feeling similar to Longstreet's, the feeling that you must spend the men like gold coins, one at a time. There are no replacements. He also has pride in his unit for its defense yesterday.

Even with all the carnage that did take place at Gettysburg, human kindness is left in some of the men — most could just not bring themselves to use their bayonets on another man. There is hope for the human race after all. And there is a sense of camaraderie and respect for fellow soldiers, regardless of what side they are on.

The Union Army needs changes in management; in fact, after this battle, changes were made. Instead of depending solely on volunteers whose enlistments ran out just when you needed them most, or fighting a unit until everyone was dead, the Union set up a draft system.

Literary Device

Ironically enough, the 20th Maine is being sent to rest in the "Safest place on the battlefield . . . in the center of the line." That is the very place Lee will attack that day. In actual historical accounts, this is not the way it happened, but putting Chamberlain there was Shaara's way of keeping his viewpoint character right in the middle of the action.

Friday, July 3, 1863
2. Longstreet

Summary

Goree returns from scouting the area. The road to Washington is still open, but the Union cavalry is closing in on Longstreet's right side. Longstreet extends Hood's division to cover that area. At least the rainy morning will help screen the movements to get Pickett's men in line for a charge.

Lee arrives and rides with Longstreet to look over the front. Longstreet relays the reconnaissance information from Goree and tries again to convince Lee to move to the south. Lee points to the center of the Union line and says, "General, the enemy is there — and there's where I'm going to strike him."

Ewell will attack at the same time further north at Cemetery Hill, keeping those forces pinned down so that they cannot reinforce the center. All the artillery will focus on pounding the center before the men charge.

In spite of his own feelings, Longstreet speaks carefully, still not wanting to hurt Lee. He tells Lee that he lost half the strength of two divisions yesterday, Union cavalry is flanking him right now, and the whole rear of the Confederate Army will be left open if Hood's and McLaws' divisions are move forward. The Confederate line could be crushed.

In addition, three Union corps are entrenched on the ridge with plenty of good artillery and with the ability to reinforce any part of their line quickly. A frontal attack on them will be uphill over open ground, the Confederate line will be spread out over five miles and hard to coordinate, and the enemy will see their every move.

Lee integrates the information and concedes Goree is accurate, but his eyes flame at Longstreet's reticence. He tells Longstreet simply that the Union will break in the center. When Longstreet disagrees, Lee turns with a look of weariness. Longstreet is concerned and wants to touch the man, but there is no place for emotion here. Many men are going to die, and heads must be clear.

When cannons go off in the north, Lee snarls about Ewell not following orders again. But the Union is charging Ewell, a surprise Lee did not expect. Lee and Longstreet walk down into the Peach Orchard to review the front. Alexander is getting the artillery ready. Lee talks to Wofford, who was in the group yesterday that almost broke the Union line. Lee says that surely they can do it again. Wofford explains that yesterday the enemy was broken, but today they are heavily reinforced. And besides, Confederate losses were heavy yesterday. Lee is not happy with this answer. Meanwhile, at the north end of the ridge, Ewell's men are being pushed back from the trenches they won the night before.

In the background, "Bonny Blue Flag" is playing in honor of Lee. The men see Lee and rise to cheer him. They gaze at him in fatherly fashion, joke with him, show their unbroken spirit. Lee sees how high his men's morale is and is fired with the belief that they are ready for this charge and that they can break the Union line. He cannot ask these men to retreat now.

Lee decides Hood and McLaws should remain where they are to defend Longstreet's right flank. He will give Longstreet Heth's and Pender's divisions to use in an attack, along with Pickett's. That will give Longstreet three full-strength divisions. They won't attack until there has been a heavy artillery barrage on the center point. Lee adds that Stuart's men have already gone around to attack that same spot from behind. The rest of Hill's corps will follow Longstreet's three divisions. Longstreet reminds Lee it is Hancock and II Corps up ahead, and they won't run.

Longstreet speaks, deliberately looking at Lee, and tells Lee that from all his years of service he feels the attack will fail. Lee is angry. Longstreet tries once more, and Lee tells him "that's enough" and then turns away.

Since both Heth and Pender have been wounded in previous battles, Pettigrew and Trimble will lead those two divisions. Lee repeats the plan and is fired up now, radiating faith and confidence.

Riding back to his command, Longstreet's hands shake, and he struggles to control himself before facing his men. A commander must be in control in front of his men. But this is the worst situation he's ever been in. Longstreet speaks with Alexander about the artillery barrage, emphasizing that the artillery must drive the Union men off the hill.

He subtly implies that Alexander must judge whether the artillery has succeeded so that the attack can begin. Longstreet then meets with Pickett, Pettigrew, and Trimble to lay out the plan. Pickett is excited; Pettigrew is pale, calm, and still; Trimble is emotional and moved, grateful for the honor to do this. They go off to ready their commands. Armistead remains alone, looking out toward the Union line, and Hancock.

Longstreet, in his thoughts, sees what is going to happen as a mathematical equation. He sees what weapons will wipe out what men along the way. There won't be many left to storm the wall when they get there, and it is simple math as to how it goes from there.

Commentary

Shaara's descriptions convey moods effectively. He describes Lee arriving in the rainy mists: " . . . there was a ghostly quality in the look of him, of all his staff, ghost riders out of the past, sabers clanking . . ." In another interchange, there is no mistaking Lee's mood and emotional power: "He looked back at Longstreet for one long moment, straight into his eyes, fixing Longstreet with the black stare, the eyes of the General . . . Longstreet drew his head in, like a turtle." Without actually stating it, Shaara shows us there is no arguing with Lee.

On the other hand, Shaara uses some very jarring shifts in point of view. At the end of this chapter, Longstreet is in agony. The last paragraph starts with Longstreet closing his eyes and then suddenly shifts to Fremantle and what he is thinking. While these shifts are infrequent in the book, they are disorienting when they appear.

Shaara also portrays Lee and Longstreet's father-son relationship: When Lee stares him down, Longstreet reacts like a child admonished by a stern father. Longstreet both needs to receive Lee's paternal nurturing and needs to take care of Lee. He is afraid of displeasing the man, and at the same time, has a deep concern for Lee's health and well-being. Longstreet will not abandon Lee even though he wants to quit.

In this chapter, Longstreet is in an emotional bind. He can barely contain his anger and despair at having to order men to their deaths, deaths he feels are preventable and useless, and deaths that happen in an attack he totally disagrees with. Longstreet wants to resign, but he won't leave Lee alone or with the attack in the hands of Hill. He is stuck in a no-win situation. Longstreet tries to shift the command responsibility to Alexander, hoping that Alexander will say "yes" or "no" to the attack based on the success of the artillery barrage. That way, Longstreet doesn't have to make the decision.

Longstreet also feels he knows how it will go. To him, there are not enough men to do this battle, and the enemy is too strongly entrenched. He can see when and how the different enemy weapons will take out large numbers of men, until few are left to storm wall. It is simple mathematics. And with Hancock up there . . . "We will lose it here."

Lee, on the other hand, is determined to attack in spite of Longstreet's input or Wofford's comments about a reinforced enemy. Instead, Lee hears his men — their jokes, their comments — and he sees their high spirits. Their morale convinces Lee to attack. Lee will attack that hill because his men believe they can do it, and *that* is his most powerful weapon.

Once Lee has done all he can, he states that it's all in God's hands, and he is content with that. Longstreet isn't. He does not think a God is listening, and even if one is, he does not feel it is God sending those men up that hill to their deaths. Longstreet concludes that maybe God wants it to work this way, but the men will die, and the South will lose it here.

There is no question Fremantle is a happy and pleasant man to have along on this campaign, and his heart is in the right place. But he is so lost in dreams of saber charges that he will never be capable of objectively assessing situations and reading them correctly. When he sees the completely agonized Longstreet, Fremantle wrongly concludes Longstreet is the master of calmness, resting before battle.

Glossary

pont au feu bridge of fire/ feu d'enfer: fire(s) of hell: Lee's way of describing the intense artillery pounding he will order on the center of the Union line to pave the way for Longstreet's attack there.

Friday, July 3, 1863

3. Chamberlain

Summary

Coming down off Little Round Top escorted by a young lieutenant named Pitzer, Chamberlain and his men can see the whole army spread out along the ridge and up to the hills at the north end. He hears about yesterday's charge by the 1st Minnesota. It attacked the Rebel line on a moment's notice at Hancock's order and bought time for reinforcements to move up. This saved the Union line when it was breaking, but out of 300 men, only 40 came back.

Pitzer tells Chamberlain that Meade wanted to pull out last night, but the rest of officers voted to stay. Pitzer adds that Hancock believes the Rebels will attack again, and it will be right in the middle of the Union line.

Chamberlain's group is placed in reserve behind Meade's headquarters. He sends one of his men to scrounge for rations while Tom checks on Kilrain at the hospital. Chamberlain is called to see General Sykes, and a sympathetic lieutenant lends him a horse to ride over.

Sykes is curt, short-tempered, and not personable, but impressed with Chamberlain's charge yesterday. He, too, comments on Chamberlain's not being regular army. Sykes will look into making Chamberlain a brigade commander. He sits there eating chicken and pickles in front of Chamberlain and never offers him anything, but he agrees to send a lieutenant to get Chamberlain's men some rations.

Chamberlain, now without the horse, must walk back to his men on his injured foot, which is burning like fire. He manages to overcome his pride and asks for help when Lieutenant Frank Haskell approaches him. Haskell kindly gets him some chicken, eyes Chamberlain with respect, and mentions he recognized Chamberlain's name. Chamberlain eats one piece of chicken and gives the other two to his men.

Tom returns, glum. He recounts the terrible conditions at the hospital and tells Chamberlain that Kilrain is dead. It wasn't his wounds; his heart just gave out.

At that moment, the battle starts with an artillery barrage. Everyone ducks for cover, and Chamberlain notes that he "had been under artillery before but never like this." He huddles against the ground and falls asleep. Chamberlain continues to wake and sleep, with everything having a surreal nature to it.

Commentary

Chamberlain notes that the 1st Minnesota had worse casualties than his own group. He reflects that during a fight your own experience always seems the worst, but to remember that others often have it worse. Chamberlain is able to objectively look at himself, notice his own flaws and pettiness, and make changes.

Chamberlain and his men are confronted with the smells of coffee, cooking chicken, and rotting dead horses. Ordinarily, the last one would kill a person's interest in the first two. But war has a way of bringing things down to raw basics. After so many hours of no food, no water, and so much exhaustion, Chamberlain and his men search for food despite the smell of dead horses.

Character Insight

The word dreamyly has shown up repeatedly throughout the book. It is a reference to Chamberlain's wife and her misspelling of that word in her letters. He thinks of the word time and again, and it is his connection to her in the middle of horror and chaos.

Chamberlain notes General Gibbon at headquarters and remembers the man has brothers serving on the other side. He wonders how many are out there today facing them. He reflects on using his own brother to fill a hole in the line — a correct command move — but "Some things a man cannot be asked to do. Killing of brothers." He realizes the whole war is about killing brothers, and he decides that will not happen in his family. Tom has to go, but Chamberlain will tell him at the right time.

After Kilrain dies, Chamberlain reflects on whether there is a heaven or not. While he mostly believes in heaven and that there should be more than just the metallic end, silence, and the worms for dead soldiers, he cannot believe in heaven at this moment. The pain of Kilrain being gone is too strong. There is only the feeling that death is just a vast dark, a huge nothing. This is how most people react. There is the theoretical belief in heaven, and happiness for the dead resting in peace, and there is the reality that crashes in when someone close dies. All you feel is the pain and emptiness. It is hard to feel that theoretical joy.

It has been said that pain and fear intensify one's senses and focus. During the intense artillery barrage, Chamberlain "stared very hard for a moment at a circle of greenish dried moss, the fine gray grain of the rock the most vivid thing he had ever seen, what marvelous eyesight one has now . . ." Ordinarily, a person wouldn't even notice such things. But the fear generated by such a barrage suddenly magnifies the small things usually overlooked.

The same thing happens when Chamberlain learns of Kilrain's death. Up to that moment, Chamberlain is feeling exhausted, hungry, and dull from pain and loss of blood. He's barely conscious. Yet when his brother tells him Kilrain is dead, Chamberlain blinks and "The world came into focus. He could see leaves of the trees dark and sharp against the blue sky. He could smell the dead horses." The dull awareness has been blasted away by emotional pain, and suddenly every sense is felt full force.

Literary
Device

Shaara foreshadows Hancock's performance in this battle, and it's seen in the comments made by several characters. Lieutenant Pitzer tells Chamberlain that Hancock believes the Rebs will attack again, right in the middle of the Union line. Longstreet has voiced his own concerns that they are up against Hancock, and Armistead knows that Hancock is their best. Lee, convinced that Meade will have reinforced his flanks and weakened the middle, may have underestimated Hancock's leadership.

Glossary

Whitworth a type of English cannon.

Friday, July 3, 1863

4. Armistead

Summary

Armistead takes in the view while the Confederate artillery is firing. As the Union shells start to land in the Confederate lines, men hide in the grass waiting to attack. Armistead checks on his men. All around him shells are landing, men are dying. In between the explosions, one can hear the band playing. Needing a private moment, Armistead goes off by himself. He sees Pickett writing a poem to his beloved, and Armistead thinks of his wife, of that last night with her, Hancock, and the song they sang. Walking over to Pickett, Armistead gives him the ring from his finger. "Here, George, send her this. My compliments."

Armistead goes back to his thoughts. He has the thoughts of a man about to meet fate and reviewing it all. He expects death, but will welcome being spared. Either way, fate will decide it, and he accepts that. Garnett approaches on horseback and against orders, intends to ride into battle instead of walk. Armistead fears Garnett is arranging his death, and he tries to get Pickett to order Garnett to stay behind, but Pickett won't do that. It's a matter of honor.

The men line up, talking, joking, the band playing a polka. Armistead says good-bye to Garnett, knowing Garnett will die and it is all in God's hands now. They march through Union artillery, first blind, seeing others getting hit, and then seeing where they'll be attacking. The action moves back and forth through Armistead's eyes: looking to the front, then the sides, at Kimble, Garnett, Kemper, at the men falling, closing ranks. The artillery increases to a "great bloody hail." They cross the field, turn, and merge with other forces. They are being hit with canister shot — millions of metal balls whirring. Armistead is shot in the leg, but moves forward. Men are with him, but not many are left. Armistead knows it's all over and can't be done, but he leads them on to wall anyway. "Virginians! With me!" Almost to the wall, walking on the backs of dead men, they give the rebel yell.

Blue troops begin to break from the fence and retreat. Armistead leaps to the wall, crosses it, sees blue troops running, and then is hit in the side. He feels no pain. He looks back and sees that the fighting is over. Blue boys are everywhere, gray boys are moving back. The song runs through his head again: "It may be for years, and it may be forever." Armistead asks to see Hancock, but he's been hit, too. Armistead cringes at the thought that both of them might die. He remembers the package he sent to Mira Hancock, prays for his friend, gives the soldier a message for Hancock, and then dies.

Commentary

Even amidst a Union artillery barrage, the band keeps playing. Though it seems surreal to the reader to imagine strands of music in between shells exploding, it must have provided comfort to the men huddling on the ground. The other music that recurs in this chapter and that is charged with deep emotion is the song "Kathleen Mavourneen."

Armistead reviews his life and reflects on how he could have been more emotional, though he notes he felt emotions deeply, if just for a moment, when his wife died. He has sent his personal Bible to Mira Hancock in a package to be opened if he dies. And he gives his ring to Pickett to send to Pickett's girlfriend. Armistead remembers his vow and takes it seriously. He knows the time has come for God to determine the outcome of that vow. He is wishing it could be different, wishing it could be changed, and he is not eager to die, just like Jesus in the Garden of Gethsemane. But Armistead will accept either outcome.

Pickett is a sentimental man of grandiose emotions. He is grateful for Armistead's ring. He is emotional over the coming battle to the point that he cannot even find words to express it.

The theme of honor is seen in Garnett's actions now. Garnett is a man at peace because he is arranging his answer to Jackson's accusation of cowardice, and he welcomes this. He will ride into battle, a perfect target, and in death, his name will be cleared. Armistead tries desperately to get Longstreet or Pickett to order Garnett to stay behind, but Armistead knows they will not.

Unexpressed emotion among the men is another recurrent theme in the book. Armistead sheds tears over Garnett's certain death, but he can't show him. The two men prepare for battle, and their eyes never meet, and they avoid shaking hands. Armistead feels overwhelming emotion for Longstreet who is sitting there looking black, savage, and he wants to say something to Longstreet. But he can't.

Theme

The theme that "It's all in God's hands" runs heavily in this climactic chapter. It is Armistead's belief for himself and his prayer for Garnett and Hancock. It is Lee's belief about the battle. The outcome is preordained. They will do their duty. The rest is up to God.

Human kindness in the midst of horror is shown by the Union officer on horseback who tried to save Armistead's life by knocking him down. The officer, admiring Armistead's courage, knew that Armistead didn't stand a chance if he remained standing. It was an unsuccessful but generous and kind act, nevertheless.

Glossary

bowling balls bowling had been brought to this country by European settlers some time before the war, though at that time it was more an outdoor lawn game.

canister an artillery shell that when fired from a cannon releases hundreds of small metal balls that murderously cut through an advancing enemy line.

solid shot a solid artillery shell that explodes when it lands.

Friday, July 3, 1863

5. Longstreet

Summary

Longstreet sits watching the battle unable to think, his mind "like a room in which there has been a butchering." He tries to pray, but can't. He sits silent and immobile as men stream by him in retreat. Pickett's aide screams for help that isn't there. Garnett's horse returns, the saddle empty. Longstreet orders Pickett to retreat.

Longstreet feels horror from the loss, weariness, and monstrous disgust. It is done, he sent them, and now he would get a gun and take a walk forward. But then he sees Lee, who is riding hatless among returning men, gently consoling them, accepting blame, urging them to show good order and not let the enemy see them run.

Longstreet has had enough. He gets a horse and his aide, Sorrel, tries to stop him, but Longstreet is savage and growls at Sorrel to let go. Heading off to where the Union is forming for attack, Longstreet sees that Goree is following him and asking for orders. Longstreet's staff is there now, grabbing the horse's bridle. The battle is ending, and blue troops are pulling back.

The men begin to realize that the battle is over. Longstreet sees the Union men cheering a general, sees them raise the blue flag of Virginia — a captured battle flag — and Longstreet turns away. He heads back to camp knowing he can't even quit.

There is a new stillness tonight — no music.

Longstreet is black, thinking of all the men who died that day. Lee arrives accompanied by the still loyal men. He speaks privately to Longstreet, who is silent. Lee shows vulnerability and weakness, something Longstreet cannot resist, and Longstreet responds to Lee's request for help with the retreat. Lee recovers his strength and speaks of doing better another day.

Choking on so much death, Longstreet cannot be silent. He tells Lee he doesn't agree and feels he cannot go on leading men to die for nothing. Lee speculates on why men die, and that they die for their own reasons. Lee indicates he will go on if the men go on. After Lee goes, Longstreet walks out to the field "to say goodbye" and then orders the retreat.

Commentary

As if defeat itself isn't bad enough, seeing the Union Army cheerfully waving the battle flag of Virginia is the ultimate humiliation. That flag represented them, their pride, and their honor.

During the battle, Longstress tries to pray but cannot. There is no one there, just like when his children died. Longstreet's men are the only children and family he has left. And now they have died. So Longstreet tries to kill himself by riding into the battle.

Lee guides his men gently. When Lee comes into Longstreet's camp, it is almost a biblical scene with the dark sky, and the men surrounding him, pleading with him. Lee has a presence that they all respond to and need, and they make him larger than life. Even in defeat, he has a majesty that continues to inspire the men.

Longstreet doesn't want to forgive Lee. Yet Lee can still get to Longstreet's emotions. Lee's fatigue, his vulnerability, his shielding of his eyes to hide his emotions from view — all these things melt Longstreet in spite of his rage. When Lee tries to say something, Longstreet just tells Lee, "Never mind." Longstreet agrees to take care of things. When Lee is assured of Longstreet's help, he recovers his strength.

Why do men die? Longstreet says he cannot go on leading men to die for nothing. Lee reflects that each man dies for his own reasons, not for their commanders. Lee doubts that the outcome of the war itself ever really mattered and that God will not ask about that in the end. Lee tells Longstreet that while commanders may have no cause, soldiers do. It is the only way they ever stand a chance of winning. It is like life itself: In the end, the challenges and the outcomes are irrelevant. It is the response chosen and the quality of its execution that matters. There is nothing else.

Friday, July 3, 1863

6. Chamberlain

Summary

In the evening after the battle, Chamberlain sits alone looking out at the battlefield. He remembers the morning with green grass and beautiful wheat fields, all of those gone now.

His brother joins him and chats, trying to make sense of the whole thing. Tom keeps asking why those men were willing to fight so hard for slavery. Both brothers admire the enemy for their courage in battle, and Chamberlain reflects on the tragedy of it.

Remembering the march of the Confederate lines toward the Union position, Chamberlain feels both the beauty of the sight and the fear it inspired. He feels one with all of them, privileged to be here, and proud of them all, regardless of side. He sees no enemies here, hates no gentlemen, and considers them all equal now in God's sight. He feels a thrill at the coming battles and knows he must send his brother away. Chamberlain moves away as the thunder brings the heavy rain that will wash all the blood away.

Commentary

Aristotle spoke of real tragedy as being a state where you feel no pain, no joy, and no hatred, just enormous space and time suspended. There is a sense of this when Chamberlain thinks of what the actual battle was like. He had completely forgotten about causes or morality once the guns started firing. The reflections and feelings come later.

As Chamberlain reflects on the charge that day he decides it was the most beautiful thing he had ever seen: officers yelling, the music, the drums, shell bursts, a mile of men coming slowly, dying as they came, knowing they were coming to kill you, flags waving. He observes that even with his own fear there is the sensation of unspeakable beauty. These seem like odd comments, especially when speaking of warfare. But it catches the beliefs of the time. War and courageous men were romantic, and lines of men coming at you created strong emotions.

Character Insight

Chamberlain thinks about the appalling thrill he feels at knowing there are more battles to come. He realizes he will fight until he dies or the war ends, and he feels an incredible eagerness for the next battle. Again, these might seem like strange emotions. But it is in the war, in the army, that Chamberlain feels most alive. Perhaps it is that ability of pain and fear to create such an intense focus that draws Chamberlain to the field of battle and makes him feel so alive. There is also the sense of history he feels a part of. Chamberlain decides he must come back to this place after the war is over to try to understand it all. The only thing he is sure of now is that he has had a privilege most men will never have. These memories will stay with him to the end of his days.

Chamberlain also reflects back to his discussion with Kilrain about men and divine spark. He concludes Kilrain's bitterness is wrong. Instead, he feels pride for the men who attacked, as if they were his own men and he was with them. He feels pity for their loss and believes that all are equal now in sight of God.

At the end of the novel, Tom sums up the confusion that others felt then and now. What *were* they fighting for? Was it really necessary to fight? So many died, and a good portion of them probably never even knew why.

Theme

The men in this story have a hard time expressing their emotions. Longstreet feels deep emotions for Armistead, Lee, his men, and his wife, but cannot show them. Chamberlain feels deep love for Tom, but cannot show it. Armistead had the same problem with his feelings for Longstreet. It is hard to know whether this is the way men were at that time, or whether the pressures of command or the pain of the war itself caused them to be this way. Perhaps if men had been able to speak to each other more, battle would have been unnecessary.

Literary Device

The motif of rain is used as a symbol for cleansing and rebirth. The rains come, wash away the blood and evidence of death, clearing the way for new life.

Afterword

This chapter summarizes what happens to a number of the participants after the battle. Lee, for example, asks to be relieved of command, but Davis won't accept it. Longstreet's resignation to Lee is also denied.

Essentially, no one is left unaffected by this battle, and some will never be the same. As the battle is later recognized as a turning point in the war, it is also a turning point for many of the men who fought there, a life-altering event, a moment in time that will mark these men throughout history.

CHARACTER ANALYSES

Robert E. Lee

Lee is a gentleman, a man of honor, and a religious man with no vices and considerable patience. Optimistic and idealistic, he believes his men can do anything. He is soft-spoken and cares about his men, but is willing to use them boldly and lose them for the Cause. He believes deeply in his God and feels God is controlling the course of events.

The Lee in this novel frequently comes across as a near zealot, blindly going forward in spite of the possible better advice of Longstreet and others. While Lee was a strong commander who didn't waver in his decisions, casting him as rigid and obsessed may not be totally accurate. Many essays and books offer logical support and reasons for Lee's decisions here.

Even within this story, Lee struggles with decisions and considers all possibilities before picking a course of action. In fact, throughout this battle, Lee constantly rethinks his plans to offset changes in circumstances, errors made by his commanders, or his orders being disobeyed. He is not rigidly attached to any plan if another will achieve his goal.

Lee is a risk-taker, makes chancy and daring decisions, and even breaks the rules because time is against him. The North can outlast him in men and supplies. Also, his health problems show up in the story and are a reminder that he may not last the war. So he is determined to fight at Gettysburg if at all possible and not retreat.

Virginia is Lee's first priority. For him, Virginia *is* the Confederacy, and he is involved in this war on the Confederate side only because his home state of Virginia chose to leave the Union. His decisions of where to attack and why are based on his loyalties.

Lee favors offensive Napoleonic warfare tactics and despises defensive strategies. He also despises the use of paid spies. His command style is loose, which is good, as he trusts his men to execute their orders without him micromanaging. It is bad because his complete trust in his men results in disappointments, such as Stuart being out of touch with Lee for several critical days, leaving Lee blind in enemy territory.

Also, an invasion of this sort so far from home, with plans of such grand scale, requires tight control and flawless communication. Lee issues no written orders, some of his orders are confusing, and he never gets all his generals together in one place to coordinate planning. This lack of organization is a downfall, especially with new commanders in place after Jackson's death.

Lee's men hold him in high esteem. They view him as nearly a god and will do anything he asks. Even when the battle fails, his men do not blame him and are ready to fight some more.

Longstreet is important to Lee. He values Longstreet for his strength, experience, and friendship. With the death of Jackson, Lee looks for the company and support of a veteran commander he can depend on.

James Longstreet

Though he is not a Virginian, Longstreet is held in high regard by Lee. A moody man with strong opinions and deep emotions, Longstreet's three children died the previous winter, all in one week, and he is tormented by enormous grief. He is pained for his wife, who also suffers much grief and to whom he has been unable to offer any emotional support. He keeps a tight emotional hold on himself, avoiding any thoughts about his family except in "alone" moments. He struggles to keep his drinking in line.

Longstreet is consumed with anger and frustration over this battle. He is certain it is a mistake and disagrees totally with Lee's offensive approach. Longstreet, instead, favors finding a strong defensive position and making the enemy come to him. He is not a coward, but bases his opinions on years of army experience, some of it out West dealing with the Indians. He is a total soldier, professional, and devoted to no cause except victory. His flaws may be inflexibility toward other approaches and a lack of vision for a gamble. His grief over the deaths of his children also may be heavily impacting his ability to function as a commander.

Longstreet has strongly conflicting feelings for Lee. Longstreet respects Lee, is friends with him, and even needs him as a father figure. At the same time, he strongly disagrees with Lee's strategy, resents Lee's decisions, and feels much rage toward Lee as his men die in battle. Yet as angry as Longstreet is with Lee, he cannot pull away from him. Longstreet still worries about Lee's health, is always respectful in his comments, and dutifully helps Lee retreat from the battle after the loss.

Longstreet is a man of deep emotions, although he shows little on the surface. He loves his men and strives hard not to waste their lives. They are family to him. He protects Pickett and has a soft spot for the man, probably out of gratitude for Pickett's help when his children died.

Longstreet enjoys Armistead, but is jealous of Armistead's friendship with the Union general Hancock. And Longstreet despises the flamboyant Stuart and the ambitious Early.

Joshua Lawrence Chamberlain

Chamberlain is an unusual man, a college professor turned regiment commander, and he views the war and the people around him more as a philosopher than a military man. He senses that they are making history and understands the importance of what they are doing. He is at home wherever he is and feels that home is not North or South, but within. He is fair and unbiased, even with the enemy. As they march toward Gettysburg and Chamberlain sees rows of dead Confederates from a previous battle, he wonders whether the local people will give them a decent burial or leave them for the buzzards. On the other hand, he cannot understand the Southerners who speak of their slaves as cattle. To Chamberlain, all men are equal, and each possesses a "divine spark" that makes a man.

With regard to army life itself, despite the discomforts, dangers, and inconveniences, Chamberlain loves it. Chamberlain is similar to Lee in many respects — he cares about his men in a fatherly way, yet he doesn't hesitate to use them, including his own brother, for the sake of the higher good — the Cause. He is idealistic, optimistic, and has faith and pride in his men. He treats them intelligently and with respect, and they in turn respond. The army is his family, his men are his children, and his aide, Kilrain, is his "father."

His own family relationships seem a bit strange. He doesn't speak much in the story about missing his children, and though he reflects on missing his wife, and no doubt there is physical longing, other than that, he seems happier away from home. He observes that "away from her you loved her more" and that while she is the only thing missing here, otherwise, this life in this army is everything he wants. It is here he feels most alive and connected to others. He is thrilled by battle — the sight of thousands of soldiers marching in formation to attack with flags waving — and he wonders how he will ever deal with going home. Though he hates to admit it, he is eager for future battles and knows he will stay until he dies or the war ends.

John Buford

Buford is a brilliant cavalry commander, dedicated, with lots of experience. He is a good "gut" commander who can read a situation and act quickly. Years out West dealing with Indians have taught him to "feel" his enemy's presence, sense what his enemy is doing, and use what his enemy has overlooked. This is evident when Buford repels the first Confederate attacks. Buford can feel what Heth is doing and is amused and elated when Heth fails to do the things a good commander should have done. Buford is quick to capitalize on the opportunity.

At least in this book, Buford is seen as a loner, weary of war and bureaucratic leaders. He avoids getting to know young lieutenants because too many of them die quickly. In reality, he was actually very close to his men, knew them all personally, took an interest in their families, and later died in the arms of one of his men.

In this book, Buford's messages to his commanders are brief and to the point. This makes for good dramatic tension. The real Buford was actually very thorough in his reports, sending lengthy messages that included location names, numbers, and as many details as he could learn.

Buford is shown as a creative commander, taking what little he has for men and supplies and making the most of them. His creativity includes using any and all weapons at his disposal. While he did arm his men with breech-loading rifles instead of muskets, the real Buford, unlike the character here, did not consider sabers or dragoon pistols silly if the situation warranted them. Sabers do not run out of bullets, and pistols work best in close-range fighting. Shaara uses his character's disdain of these tools as a dramatic way of reinforcing a distaste for gentlemen.

Like the book character, the real Buford despised the "false flourish," so characteristic of gentility. Colonel Charles Wainwright, a 1st Corps artillery chief, noted at Buford's death that the cavalry commander was similar to Reynolds, "being rough in his exterior, never looking after his own comfort, untiring on the march . . . quiet and unassuming in his manners."

CRITICAL ESSAYS

History or Novel?

Michael Shaara opens *The Killer Angels* with a note to the reader and explains that while he "condensed some of the action . . . eliminated some minor characters . . . had to choose between conflicting viewpoints," he did not knowingly violate the action or consciously change any fact. He also notes that the interpretation of the characters is his own. While Shaara no doubt strove to preserve the "spirit" of the action, the very act of interpreting and adjusting things for dramatic effect makes the story fiction.

D. Scott Hartwig, author of *A Killer Angels Companion*, sums up the dilemma: "Shaara's story is told so well, his character portrayals so believable, that the unknowing reader might believe what they are reading *is* history." Hartwig, Donald C. Pfanz, Glenn Tucker, and others who have studied Gettysburg in great detail, show through their writings that the novel and facts differ in a number of places. *The Killer Angels* is a great work of historical fiction, but fiction is not and never will be history itself.

The Battle of Gettysburg — the Civilian Experience

Little is said in the novel about the civilians in the Gettysburg area and how the battle affected them. However, this battle did not take place in isolation; it had a devastating effect on the people living there.

During the battle, inhabitants of Gettysburg hid in their houses, often in basements. They generally did not venture upstairs until night because it wasn't safe. In fact, reports tell of women killed by stray bullets while baking in their kitchens.

Many of the inhabitants risked death by hiding Union soldiers trapped behind Confederate lines after the Union retreat through Gettysburg. Those soldiers had to remain hidden for the three days of the battle, while the Confederates searched residences to find them. Protecting the Union soldiers required courage and creativity.

While July 4th brought the end of battle and cheers from the victorious soldiers, the after-effects of the battle would be felt for months. Out in the open, surgeons continued to amputate, embalmers worked on those that didn't make it, soldiers searched for anyone who might still be alive, and curiosity-seekers came out to gawk at the destruction and collect souvenirs. Local people took wounded into their homes, public buildings were also used as hospitals, and a tent hospital was set up on the east side of town. A number of the wounded remained in Gettysburg for several months, and the local population also took in a number of relatives who came to care for wounded soldiers.

The battlefield itself was a disaster. The original fields of wheat, barley, oats, corn, and grass became crater-marked muddy expanses with blood-filled ditches. Wounded soldiers groaned as they waited in pouring rain and blistering sun to be rescued.

The hospitals were no better than the battlefield, except that some of the men got some medical care, some coffee, and a cracker or two. Otherwise, their hospital beds were the muddy hillsides, with no tents, blankets, fires, or water. Many of the men waited days for any care, and those with severe head injuries were often set aside to die as the surgeons could do nothing for them.

Graves were hurriedly dug to deal with the decomposing bodies. Given that thousands were killed, there was little time to bury them properly. Instead, 50 to 100 bodies were lined up in rows, the Confederates in one row, and the Union soldiers in another. They were then buried in trenches three feet deep and seven feet wide. Unfortunately, these trenches were often dug up by farmers hurriedly plowing new crops or by hogs and other animals rooting around for food. It would be a long time before the bodies were either removed for proper burial elsewhere, or a national cemetery could be established. Gettysburg would never be the same, and neither would its inhabitants.

Good versus Evil; Man versus Challenge

Shaara weaves a complex story with many themes and motifs. The struggles include large, life-altering ones: good versus evil; man against himself, his environment, or his opponent; and small mundane ones, such as how the lack of shoes started a major battle.

Someone once said that all themes are really about good against evil. If that is so, this novel shows that the outcome of good versus evil is not a black or white answer. Good people make bad decisions, questionable people perform heroically, and great victories occur in the midst of miserable situations. Shaara does not make one side good and the other bad, and no character is cast as the ultimate villain. They are all just men, imperfect men, struggling to do their best in a bad situation.

If there is any evil or villain in this story, it is circumstance — the war, the differences of opinion, the changing technology of weapons, the physical conditions, the miscommunications. Were it not for circumstance, many of these men currently on opposite sides would be united as family or sharing a drink as friends.

Essentially, who or what man battles, or even how those battles turn out, is irrelevant. The main theme of this novel is about how one responds to challenges . . . to life itself. There are any number of struggles in this story, and any number of enemies in life. The ultimate question is How will you face them? What choices will you make, and why? Things such as duty, honor, freedom, dignity, spirit, pride, courage, and determination all play a role in the outcome, and Shaara demonstrates this with his characters.

Questions as Theme

If another theme could be summed up in one word, it would be the question "Why?" The very fact that one of the major themes is a question is itself significant. It is a statement about war and about life. In both, there are more questions than answers. Life is uncertain. War is unfair. Both are confusing and at the mercy of things beyond your control. Ultimately, the only thing you can control is your reaction to it all. Based on who you are and what you feel, you make a choice of how to respond. Everything else is beyond our control, a question left in the hands of fate.

Some of the "whys" include:

Why write this book? The author mirrors the thoughts of Stephen Crane who explained that he wrote *Red Badge of Courage* because he "wanted to know what it was like to be there, what the weather was like, what men's faces looked like. In order to live it, he had to write it."

Shaara describes the heat of the day, the geography of the land, what the dust feels like on their faces as they march. He relates smells of death, sounds of battle, images of destroyed bodies. You see what they eat, what their clothes look like, and all the focused details that bring the reader into that place to "live" it.

Why explore that place? Through stories, you can magnify a portion of life, examine it in detail, and hope to understand something about it. In the struggles of a story, you see the struggles of your life. If you find answers to the problems of a story, you find answers to something about life. An immense story about a bloody battle with its extremes of emotion, conflict, and action may provide answers to some of the larger and more universal questions everyone faces.

Why the particular framework, events, and people? The framework allows the author to tell the story through the words and emotions of the men themselves. By fictionalizing the characters, Shaara can use their words, deeds, and thoughts to make them real and meaningful.

Shaara indicates that he avoided using any historical or military commentaries on the battle when he researched the novel. He wanted, instead, to feel it through the people that were there, so he used their letters and personal documents as sources.

The events selected are a result of the characters Shaara focuses on. Gettysburg was a huge battle with thousands of participants and hundreds of things happening at once. To try to show them all would make it impossible for the reader to feel any personal or emotional connection.

Instead, Shaara picks a few key characters to represent and portray the struggles, emotions, and story of the entire battle. The characters he chooses show the battle from both sides, from all levels of command, and from the sidelines as well as the middle of the fighting.

Why is this battle being fought? This theme is introduced in the first chapter, when you find out that Longstreet does not agree with the invasion. This thread runs through the entire book, affecting decisions and actions, especially those of Longstreet and Lee. It is a major source of conflict between the two men and is one of the biggest conflicts of the story itself.

The decision for the battle came in May 1863 when Lee and President Davis met in Richmond to discuss where the Confederate Army should focus next. Davis felt the West needed attention, especially Vicksburg, which was in danger from General Grant's troops. However, Lee felt it essential to keep up the pressure on the North, especially by attacking them on their own ground.

Many considered it risky, but Lee understood he could not hope to outlast the Union Army in terms of men or supplies. His philosophy was to strike boldly and offensively with a quick series of battles that would demoralize the Union. He felt that if he could win a decisive battle up North, the Union would quickly tire of the war and press for peace. Much discussion concerning the wisdom of Lee's plan has occurred, but nevertheless, he prevailed.

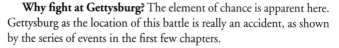

Why fight at Gettysburg? The element of chance is apparent here. Gettysburg as the location of this battle is really an accident, as shown by the series of events in the first few chapters.

The various army units of both sides are moving in the same direction. They end up dangerously close to each other, a fact neither side realizes until the last minute, when the conflict starts.

Why fight the Civil War? The Cause of the Civil War is another major theme in the book. The Southern understanding of the Cause is much different than most people's assumptions. To the men of the Confederacy, it is not about slavery. In fact, Lee himself has no slaves and does not believe in the institution. It is instead about freedom, about preserving the right of states to manage their own affairs and way of life. It is what we fought for in the American Revolution. In a lot of respects, if the Civil War is viewed with the same mindset as the Revolution, a case could be made for Jefferson Davis being right. Unfortunately for the South, everyone else perceives it to be about slavery, and this misperception prevents the South from obtaining much needed foreign help.

The Cause from the Northern perspective is revealed through the conversations and thoughts of Chamberlain and his men. The ironic thing to note here is that the North is also fighting for freedom. But it is freedom of the individual, not the state. The North is fighting for freedom from slavery, freedom to become whatever you can by your own hard work.

Shaara uses these differences in beliefs to characterize the people in his story. Lee's men will follow him anywhere for their Cause. Longstreet has no use for one. Chamberlain is nearly a zealot for his. These personal reactions define the people involved.

The reactions also show the sense of confusion and misunderstanding about the whole war. There is a sadness to it all. One has the feeling as the story progresses that if the two sides could have sat down calmly and really listened to each other, they might have heard a similar thing and worked out a peaceful solution. It only intensifies the sense of waste one feels by the end of the book over so much bloodshed and death.

Why call it The Killer Angels? The title originates with an incident in Chamberlain's childhood. Quoting Shakespeare to his father one day, Chamberlain delivers the lines, "What a piece of work is man . . . in action how like an angel." When his father reflects that if man is an angel he must be a murdering one, Chamberlain is inspired to prepare an oration for school on "Man, the Killer Angel."

Later, in conversations with Kilrain, a former sergeant in his regiment who is like a father to him, Chamberlain discusses his thoughts on the nature of man. Chamberlain sees each man as equal, possessing a "divine spark" that separates him from animals. Chamberlain is an idealist who still sees man as an angel. Kilrain, however, sees many a man as having no more worth than a dead dog.

At the end of the story, as he looks out over the field of dead bodies, Chamberlain remembers Kilrain's words and thinks back on Killer Angels. Chamberlain realizes he cannot agree, feeling strongly connected to all the men that day, regardless of side. He concludes instead that at least in the sight of God, they are all equal now.

Emotions/Beliefs

The era of the Civil War was a time of strongly held beliefs, deep emotions, and grandiose actions. By today's standards, some of it may seem trite or excessive, but for that time, it was sincere. Some of the themes in this area are

Class structure: Class distinctions are very strong, especially in the South. It is an aristocratic structure where gentlemen are an exclusive club, and to be a Virginian is the best. They are refined, wealthy, powerful, and ruled by a code of chivalry. Honor is everything, and a man would die to save or recover his honor. This theme figures prominently in many of the Southern characters in the story, especially Armistead, Garnett, and Pickett. It is also something the Englishman, Fremantle, recognizes at once and admires for its closeness to England.

The North is just the opposite. The class constraints of the Old World are despised and rejected. Instead, the culture is composed of immigrants seeking freedom from that world. They want only the chance to be judged for who they are and what they can do, not who their father was. The character of Kilrain portrays this very strongly, as does Buford, whose comments and observations about "gentlemen" and their methods of battle, are laced with sarcasm.

Glory of battle: Men of this time speak with great emotion of the glory of battle. They recall fondly the Charge of the Light Brigade. They revel in saber charges and speak passionately about the beauty of thousands of brave men in formation marching to their deaths, with banners flying and music playing. They are fearless men performing daring exploits for the glory of their cause and their homes.

Rebel Yell: The Confederates have a blood-curling yell they use as they attack. It is meant to inspire the men on to glory and strike terror into the hearts of their opponents.

Flags: A point of honor is the flag or pennant carried by a particular group in battle. The flag helps to keep things organized during the chaos of a fight. Men can look to the flag and see where they are supposed to be. But it is also an emotional tool, a metaphor for success or failure. Men would die rather than let their banner fall, and it is a great loss of honor to have one's banner captured. It is an equal honor to capture as many of the enemy's flags as possible.

Music: Music was used in camp as well as in battle. In camp, there might be sentimental singing and music, bringing thoughts of home, the past, and friends long gone. There are also the times with visiting relatives and polka bands, giving the camp a carnival atmosphere. Bugle calls and drums are used for marching and in battle to keep men in ranks, let them know where their group is, and what they are to do next.

Strategy: Strategy is mentioned frequently throughout the book. Lee prefers Napoleonic tactics, which is the currently favored method of fighting in the world, and ties into honor. One does not gain glory or honor sitting behind defensive works. Longstreet takes up the opposite position, preferring defensive strategies that make the enemy come to him. He advocates the use of trenches, something Lee refuses to do. Lee sees the Napoleonic method as an extension of the man, and that is the only way he will fight. Most of the Southern officers and Fremantle agree with Lee.

Interestingly, the Union cavalry commander, Buford, seems to agree with Longstreet's beliefs. Both of the men have served out West and value defensive tactics as much, if not more than, the flamboyant charges of offensive warfare. To this day, there remains the question of whether the loss at Gettysburg was due to Lee's poor judgment and refusal to consider a different strategy, or Longstreet's lack of commitment because he disagreed with the strategy Lee was using.

God's will: The book has a strong element of "predestination" and of "God's will at work" in the battle. Lee speaks frequently of forces beyond all of them directing the battle and that all of it is in God's hands.

It also has the element of divine retribution for a sacred oath broken. All the Confederate officers who had earlier served in the Union Army took an oath to protect and preserve the Union. That oath was broken when they took up arms for the Confederacy. In discussions between Lee and Longstreet, you see that they harbor doubts about whether they were right to break that oath, and whether that betrayal will cost them the war. Even the wife of General Pender predicts her husband will die because the Confederates have moved onto Union soil, and the Lord will avenge that.

Other elements to watch for in the book include Shaara's use of character, relationships, and irony, as well the themes of command style conflicts, command mistakes, morale in the two armies, the effect of chance and circumstance in the battle, and the issue of "good ground."

The Lee versus Longstreet Battle Strategy Conflict

Longstreet's invention of trench warfare is mentioned as new and innovative in the book, but trenches had been used since days of the Romans. In fact, Lee had used trenches himself and would do so again in future battles.

Longstreet was a strong proponent of the tactical defensive in warfare, a good idea in the right situation, such as at Fredericksburg. However, there is no one formula for success. Whereas Lee was constantly adjusting his strategy to accommodate new developments, Longstreet offered no such flexibility.

Also, it is a lot harder to be the person in charge and ultimately responsible. Longstreet, for all of his military talents, may have been better in a supporting role than in the lead one. For example, in a later campaign in Tennessee, Longstreet suffered one of the most complete repulses that the Army of Northern Virginia ever experienced in the war. He tried to shift the blame to others and commented to an aide that "he preferred being under General Lee, as it relieved him of responsibility and assured confidence." So the Longstreet of real life may not have been as perfect as the one here in the story.

Lee understood the merit of Longstreet's idea to swing around the Union Army to get between them and Washington. However, Lee decided on Gettysburg, not out of an uncontrollable emotional zeal, but because it was the safest and best choice given the circumstances he faced. Lee knew very little about the enemy's location and strength. He knew only that two of the seven Union corps were in front of him, leaving five unaccounted for at that point. Without Jeb Stuart to scope things out and lead him safely around the Union Army, Lee and his men risked stumbling into larger Union forces by accident. Since this is precisely what happened with Heth's forces on July 1, precipitating the whole battle, Lee was most likely eager not to repeat that mistake.

Again, there are countless writings on the subject analyzing it from all sides. In the end, Lee made the decision he did based on what he thought was best at the moment. Second-guessing by subordinates who didn't bear the responsibility for the decision, or Monday-morning quarterbacking, is always easier.

Certainly, Lee may have been wrong, and Longstreet right. General Eisenhower, when questioned about his opinion of Lee's tactics at Gettysburg, commented, "Why he didn't go around there [Little Round Top], I'll never know." And Eisenhower, responding to General Montgomery, who commented that he'd never have fought the battle the way Lee did, said, "If you had, I'd have sacked you." So there are certainly modern military experts who had doubts about Lee's choices, adding fuel to the idea suggested by the novel that Lee was obsessed with attacking at all costs.

However, it has also been noted that General George Patton's bold thrusts in World War II with his Third Army were the direct result of studying Lee's methods. Was Lee mad to stay and fight, or was he correct given the facts he had at the moment? The bottom line is that it is a very subjective question, and the portrayal in this novel is weighted heavily in Longstreet's favor. The reader needs to be aware that this may or may not be right and not to accept the novel's portrayal as the final word on the subject.

CliffsNotes Review

Use this CliffsNotes Review to test your understanding of the original text, and reinforce what you've learned in this book. After you work through the essay questions, you're well on your way to understanding a comprehensive and meaningful interpretation of *The Killer Angels*.

Essay Questions

1. Should Lee have been at Gettysburg?

2. What other options, if any, did Lee have and why did he choose Gettysburg?

3. What might have happened if Lee listened to Longstreet and went south around the Union Army instead of attacking at Gettysburg?

4. Was the Civil War about slavery at all?

5. How did the continual changes in Union command structure affect its army's performance, morale, training, battlefield decisions?

6. Did Jeb Stuart's lack of contact with Lee contribute to the loss at Gettysburg? Had he stuck closer to Ewell, could the battle have turned out differently?

7. Was Ewell wrong not to take Cemetery Hill the first day of the battle?

CliffsNotes Resource Center

The learning doesn't need to stop here. CliffsNotes Resource Center shows you the best of the best — links to the best information in print and online about the author and/or related works. And don't think that this is all we've prepared for you; we've put all kinds of pertinent information at www.cliffsnotes.com. Look for all the terrific resources at your favorite bookstore or local library and on the Internet. When you're online, make your first stop www.cliffsnotes.com where you'll find more incredibly useful information about *The Killer Angels*.

Books

This CliffsNotes book provides a meaningful interpretation of *The Killer Angels*. If you are looking for information about the author and/or related works, check out these other publications:

Gettysburg and the Civil War:

The Battle of Gettysburg, by Harry W. Pfanz, former National Park Service chief historian, and Scott Hartwig, Chief Historian at the Gettysburg National Military Park. This book gives an excellent overview of the events leading to this battle, as well as a thorough summary of the battle itself. Part of the Civil War Series. Conshohocken, Pa.: Eastern National, 1994.

Gettysburg: Culp's Hill and Cemetery Hill, by Harry W. Pfanz, gives an excellent account of the crucial first day battles for the "good ground." Edited by Gary W. Gallagher. Chapel Hill: University of North Carolina Press, 1993.

Gettysburg: The Second Day, by Harry W. Pfanz, is a thorough telling of the events on both sides during the second day of battle. Chapel Hill: University of North Carolina Press, 1987.

Gettysburg: A Battlefield Atlas, by Craig L. Symonds, contains excellent maps of the battle's progress as well as detailed summaries of the battle action and groups involved. Baltimore: The Nautical & Aviation Publishing Company of America, 1992.

Gods and Generals, by Jeff Shaara, is the first book of the Civil War trilogy. It precedes *The Killer Angels,* written by Jeff's father. 1996. Reprint, New York: Ballantine Books, 1997.

A Killer Angels Companion, by D. Scott Hartwig, gives an excellent account of where history and fiction part ways in this book. Gettysburg: Thomas Publications, 1996.

The Last Full Measure, also by Jeff Shaara, is the last book in the above trilogy. New York: Ballantine Books,1998.

It's easy to find books published by IDG Books Worldwide, Inc. and other publishers. You'll find them in your favorite bookstores (on the Internet and at a store near you). We also have three Web sites that you can use to read about all the books we publish:

■ www.cliffsnotes.com

■ www.dummies.com

■ www.idgbooks.com

Internet

Check out these Web resources for more information about the Battle of Gettysburg:

The Battle of Gettysburg Interactive Battle Tour, users.lr.net/~duda/home.html, has an overview of the battle and its leaders and an excellent set of interactive maps for each day of the battle. Click the maps to access additional information.

The **Battlefield Maps** page of **Gettysburg.com**, www.gettysburg.com/bog/batmaps1.htm, The Official Web Site of the Gettysburg Convention and Visitors Bureau, has maps detailing the movement of troops in 1863 and modern maps of the Gettysburg National Military Park.

Gettysburg Discussion Group Web page, www.gdg.org/, provides information on the discussion group, which is open to anyone with an interest in the 1863 battle. The page also has articles by National Park Service Historians, book reviews, and links to related sites.

Gettysburg National Military Park On The Web, www.nps.gov/gett/home.htm, is the National Park Service Gettysburg historical site listing background information, current information about visiting Gettysburg battleground, a calendar of events and battle reenactments coming up, and a virtual online tour of the battleground.

Next time you're on the Internet, don't forget to drop by www.cliffsnotes.com. We created an online Resource Center that you can use today, tomorrow, and beyond.

Send Us Your Favorite Tips

In your quest for learning, have you ever experienced that sublime moment when you figure out a trick that saves time or trouble? Perhaps you realized you were taking ten steps to accomplish something that could have taken two. Or you found a little-known workaround that gets great results. If you've discovered a useful tip that helped you understand *The Killer Angels* more effectively and you'd like to share it, the CliffsNotes staff would love to hear from you. Go to our Web site at www.cliffsnotes.com and click the Talk to Us button. If we select your tip, we may publish it as part of CliffsNotes Daily, our exciting, free e-mail newsletter. To find out more or to subscribe to a newsletter, go to www.cliffsnotes.com on the Web.

Index

CliffsNotes

LITERATURE NOTES

Absalom, Absalom!
The Aeneid
Agamemnon
Alice in Wonderland
All the King's Men
All the Pretty Horses
All Quiet on the
    Western Front
All's Well &
    Merry Wives
American Poets of the
    20th Century
American Tragedy
Animal Farm
Anna Karenina
Anthem
Antony and Cleopatra
Aristotle's Ethics
As I Lay Dying
The Assistant
As You Like It
Atlas Shrugged
Autobiography of
    Ben Franklin
Autobiography of
    Malcolm X
The Awakening
Babbit
Bartleby & Benito
    Cereno
The Bean Trees
The Bear
The Bell Jar
Beloved
Beowulf
The Bible
Billy Budd & Typee
Black Boy
Black Like Me
Bleak House
Bless Me, Ultima
The Bluest Eye & Sula
Brave New World
The Brothers Karamazov

The Call of the Wild &
    White Fang
Candide
The Canterbury Tales
Catch-22
Catcher in the Rye
The Chosen
The Color Purple
Comedy of Errors…
Connecticut Yankee
The Contender
The Count of
    Monte Cristo
Crime and Punishment
The Crucible
Cry, the Beloved
    Country
Cyrano de Bergerac
Daisy Miller &
    Turn…Screw
David Copperfield
Death of a Salesman
The Deerslayer
Diary of Anne Frank
Divine Comedy-I.
    Inferno
Divine Comedy-II.
    Purgatorio
Divine Comedy-III.
    Paradiso
Doctor Faustus
Dr. Jekyll and Mr. Hyde
Don Juan
Don Quixote
Dracula
Electra & Medea
Emerson's Essays
Emily Dickinson Poems
Emma
Ethan Frome
The Faerie Queene
Fahrenheit 451
Far from the Madding
    Crowd
A Farewell to Arms
Farewell to Manzanar
Fathers and Sons
Faulkner's Short Stories

Faust Pt. I & Pt. II
The Federalist
Flowers for Algernon
For Whom the Bell Tolls
The Fountainhead
Frankenstein
The French
    Lieutenant's Woman
The Giver
Glass Menagerie &
    Streetcar
Go Down, Moses
The Good Earth
The Grapes of Wrath
Great Expectations
The Great Gatsby
Greek Classics
Gulliver's Travels
Hamlet
The Handmaid's Tale
Hard Times
Heart of Darkness &
    Secret Sharer
Hemingway's
    Short Stories
Henry IV Part 1
Henry IV Part 2
Henry V
House Made of Dawn
The House of the
    Seven Gables
Huckleberry Finn
I Know Why the
    Caged Bird Sings
Ibsen's Plays I
Ibsen's Plays II
The Idiot
Idylls of the King
The Iliad
Incidents in the Life of
    a Slave Girl
Inherit the Wind
Invisible Man
Ivanhoe
Jane Eyre
Joseph Andrews
The Joy Luck Club
Jude the Obscure

Julius Caesar
The Jungle
Kafka's Short Stories
Keats & Shelley
The Killer Angels
King Lear
The Kitchen God's Wife
The Last of the
    Mohicans
Le Morte d'Arthur
Leaves of Grass
Les Miserables
A Lesson Before Dying
Light in August
The Light in the Forest
Lord Jim
Lord of the Flies
The Lord of the Rings
Lost Horizon
Lysistrata & Other
    Comedies
Macbeth
Madame Bovary
Main Street
The Mayor of
    Casterbridge
Measure for Measure
The Merchant
    of Venice
Middlemarch
A Midsummer Night's
    Dream
The Mill on the Floss
Moby-Dick
Moll Flanders
Mrs. Dalloway
Much Ado About
    Nothing
My Ántonia
Mythology
Narr. …Frederick
    Douglass
Native Son
New Testament
Night
1984
Notes from the
    Underground

The Odyssey
Oedipus Trilogy
Of Human Bondage
Of Mice and Men
The Old Man and
the Sea
Old Testament
Oliver Twist
The Once and
Future King
One Day in the Life of
Ivan Denisovich
One Flew Over
the Cuckoo's Nest
100 Years of Solitude
O'Neill's Plays
Othello
Our Town
The Outsiders
The Ox Bow Incident
Paradise Lost
A Passage to India
The Pearl
The Pickwick Papers
The Picture of
Dorian Gray
Pilgrim's Progress
The Plague
Plato's Euthyphro...
Plato's The Republic
Poe's Short Stories
A Portrait of the
Artist...
The Portrait of a Lady
The Power and
the Glory
Pride and Prejudice
The Prince
The Prince and
the Pauper
A Raisin in the Sun
The Red Badge of
Courage
The Red Pony
The Return of the
Native
Richard II
Richard III

The Rise of
Silas Lapham
Robinson Crusoe
Roman Classics
Romeo and Juliet
The Scarlet Letter
A Separate Peace
Shakespeare's
Comedies
Shakespeare's Histories
Shakespeare's
Minor Plays
Shakespeare's Sonnets
Shakespeare's Tragedies
Shaw's Pygmalion &
Arms...
Silas Marner
Sir Gawain...Green
Knight
Sister Carrie
Slaughterhouse-five
Snow Falling on Cedars
Song of Solomon
Sons and Lovers
The Sound and the Fury
Steppenwolf &
Siddhartha
The Stranger
The Sun Also Rises
T.S. Eliot's Poems &
Plays
A Tale of Two Cities
The Taming of the
Shrew
Tartuffe, Misanthrope...
The Tempest
Tender Is the Night
Tess of the D'Urbervilles
Their Eyes Were
Watching God
Things Fall Apart
The Three Musketeers
To Kill a Mockingbird
Tom Jones
Tom Sawyer
Treasure Island &
Kidnapped
The Trial

Tristram Shandy
Troilus and Cressida
Twelfth Night
Ulysses
Uncle Tom's Cabin
The Unvanquished
Utopia
Vanity Fair
Vonnegut's Works
Waiting for Godot
Walden
Walden Two
War and Peace
Who's Afraid of
Virginia...
Winesburg, Ohio
The Winter's Tale
The Woman Warrior
Worldly Philosophers
Wuthering Heights
A Yellow Raft in
Blue Water

Check Out the All-New CliffsNotes Guides

TECHNOLOGY TOPICS

Balancing Your Check-
book with Quicken
Buying and Selling
on eBay
Buying Your First PC
Creating a Winning
PowerPoint 2000
Presentation
Creating Web Pages
with HTML
Creating Your First
Web Page
Exploring the World
with Yahoo!
Getting on the Internet
Going Online with AOL
Making Windows 98
Work for You

Setting Up a
Windows 98
Home Network
Shopping Online Safely
Upgrading and
Repairing Your PC
Using Your First iMac
Using Your First PC
Writing Your First
Computer Program

PERSONAL FINANCE TOPICS

Budgeting & Saving
Your Money
Getting a Loan
Getting Out of Debt
Investing for the
First Time
Investing in
401(k) Plans
Investing in IRAs
Investing in
Mutual Funds
Investing in the
Stock Market
Managing Your Money
Planning Your
Retirement
Understanding
Health Insurance
Understanding
Life Insurance

CAREER TOPICS

Delivering a Winning
Job Interview
Finding a Job
on the Web
Getting a Job
Writing a Great Resume